The Educational Heretics

Alice Miller:
The Unkind Society, Parenting and Schooling

by Chris Shute

Educational Heretics Press

Published 1994 by Educational Heretics Press
113 Arundel Drive, Bramcote Hills, Nottingham NG9 3FQ

Copyright © 1994 Educational Heretics Press

British Cataloguing in Publication Data

A catalogue record for this book is available from the British Library

Shute, Christopher

Alice Miller: the Unkind Society, Parenting and Schooling

ISBN   0-9518022-5-9

Design and production: Educational Heretics Press

Printed by Mastaprint, Sandiacre, Nottinghamshire

Contents

Foreword

1. The unkind society   1

2. Poisoned relationships   13

3. Unkind education makes unkind institutions   25

4. Unrecognised abuse   37

5. Knowledge, honesty and a healthy society   47

6. Changing things   57

Bibliography   67

Foreword

A book about another author inevitably risks being compared with that author's work. I should be impertinent if I claimed to have grasped all Alice Miller's ideas or done justice to them in this book. I am not a psychoanalyst or a professional psychologist. I am an experienced educator who has come to the conclusion that educating young people ought to be an amateur activity. I have watched countless children mishandled, manipulated and damaged for life by clever professionals who know a great deal about insinuating knowledge of their academic subjects into the minds of children, but nothing at all about responding rightly to their emotions. I have worked alongside teachers who genuinely liked their pupils but who were invariably good at blunting the edge of any strong feelings those children might have been trying to express, so that their lessons were, in appearance at least, oases of geniality and harmony in a harsh world.

They were confident that by their intelligence and the skilful way they organised their work they were doing something indispensable which would help their pupils to live useful lives. Yet, tragically, they could not recognise how they were distorting those children by preventing them, however gently, from living out their frustrated longing to be unique in an institution dedicated to conformity. I came to realise how even apparently benevolent teachers, and other adults in authority who shared their convictions and methods, were in part responsible for our society's manifest failure, for all its complexity and sophistication, to produce non-violent adults.

I had already begun to sense that something was fundamentally wrong with our educational tradition when I read Alice Miller's book *For Your Own Good*. Although she was primarily interested in the effect of abusive parenting on the later development of children, she seemed to be speaking directly to me as a teacher. I was gripped by her fearless brushing aside of traditional theories about children and her readiness to give full weight to their feelings. She rejected all the well-worn assumptions about child-nature which insisted that from their birth children are wicked, dangerous creatures who are liable to make a mess of things if adults do not bear down heavily on them. She was, unlike almost any other writer I had read on the origins and development of emotions, able to recognise and declare that children are of all people the most vulnerable. She understood how absurd it is for parents to claim, as many do, that it is they who suffer lives of constant burdensome restriction and pain, and their children who bask in a sort of carefree lotus-eating freedom. Her words struck chords in me because I remembered how as a child I had often been caught in the toils of that very absurdity. I have always been almost neurotically eager to do what was expected of me. When I was too small to have much influence on the events unfolding round me, I lived in a state of mind made up in equal parts of bewilderment and apprehension. I wanted nothing out of life but that it should let me be as safe as I could be in the midst of a World War. The nightly cowering under the stairs waiting for the All-Clear was disturbing enough, but at least the adults in my life shared the general sense of crisis and danger with me. Far worse, from my point of view, was the simple fact that every so often the world stopped whatever else it was doing, reached down, and did something painful to me.

I knew almost nothing about adults' motives and feelings. I could only conjecture that I was 'bad', and that 'badness' was some sort of disease. If the cure for that disease was browbeating and blows, I had no choice but to endure it. However, even then I possessed enough self-knowledge to be indignant, because I meant no harm to anyone. I hated being a person who could never defend or explain himself, an innocent who at any moment could be declared guilty of some fault which he did not even know was a fault, punished with arbitrary harshness, and forbidden to show any sign of the rage inside him.

Perhaps the keenness of those early feelings was what drew me to Dr. Miller's writings. I would be arrogant if I claimed that every child experienced the early stages of his life as I did, or that English methods of child-rearing were fundamentally flawed and only I knew how to mend them. I am sure, however, of one thing: when we advanced, civilised, adult Europeans talk about children and discuss among ourselves what we presume they need, we do not often ask them respectfully to tell us what is happening in their minds. We do not go to any great lengths to find out if the way they look to us is the way they really are. We behave as if our understanding were perfect and our wisdom godlike. In consequence, however hard we try to be just, loving and kind, we cannot fail at some stage in their lives to make our children angry, and to block the natural discharge of that anger because its expression disturbs us and challenges our sense of the prestige which is our due as adults. If only this element of Dr. Miller's message emerges from this book it will be enough. She explains how the source of violence in Society is not extrinsic influences acting upon people, such as violent films, pornography or computer games, but rather the experience of having to keep hidden from their parents' raw, uncompromising indignation, caused and sustained by those parents' complacent, high-minded, utterly uncomprehending running of their lives.

Chapter one

The unkind society

A few years ago, shortly after I retired from teaching, I began to read books by Alice Miller, a German psychotherapist. Her ideas gripped me because they seemed to offer a clear, logical explanation for the violence, both latent and openly expressed, which I saw in families, schools and in the wider world.

Some of Dr. Miller's most striking ideas concern **the genesis of tyranny.** In *For Your Own Good* she examines the early life of Adolf Hitler. The son of an austere, unfeeling father and an ineffectual mother, the young Adolf grew up in a community which accepted and approved of the harsh treatment of children.

Dr. Miller had received a conventional training in Freudian psychotherapy, and had for many years worked with patients in the belief that they benefited from traditional analysis. This analysis presupposed that people behaved neu-rotically because the inbuilt mechanism of drives and complexes every human being is born with had caused a conflict between them and their parents which they had not been able to resolve harmoniously.

Perhaps the most common and the best known of these conflicts was the Oedipus Complex. Freud felt that the ancient Greek myth of Oedipus was far more than a tragic story. It embodied for him the essential mechanism which drives any son to wrest his independence from his father. He saw in the image of the young Oedipus killing his father and marrying his own mother a vivid delineation of a conflict which he believed nature compels every person to fight out during his childhood.

Freud assumed that the drives which caused Oedipal conflict were innate. He passed on to his disciples and successors a conviction that parents and children could not avoid playing out their assigned roles as they grew up together. As a direct result of this assumption, Freudian analysts set themselves the goal of persuading their clients to 'come to terms' with their parents.

This meant accepting that the tension between the child and the adults who had control of him when he was too small to influence his fate was simply part of life. The client had to suppress any feelings of indignation or helpless, frustrated anger which might invade his mind when he thought about his early life. He could only be free of his neuroses, the Freudians said, if he 'resolved' his conflicts and put the whole episode to rest in the deepest places of his soul. Then, and only then, would he be free.

Dr. Miller came to a point where she could no longer accept this network of assumptions. She met an art therapist who encouraged her to draw vivid abstract pictures. Through these the therapist was able to reveal to her that she had been harbouring a dammed-up reservoir of painful emotions. Her mother had inflicted on her both emotional cruelty and sexual exploitation. Like so many other children who are hurt by their parents, Alice Miller forgot what had happened to her. Unable to defend herself or express her indignation she concealed all her anguish in an area of her mind where it could no longer intrude into her consciousness.

What else could she do? Like any child she was uniquely helpless, thrust into a world which she could not yet understand, injured in her heart by its careless cruelty but forced to go on living in it. She had not even the right which adults have when the burden of life becomes unendurable, to put their problems behind them and go somewhere else. Forgetting at least allowed her to go on.

As she learned more about the reality of her past, Dr. Miller began to look at her patients and their neuroses in a new light. It became clear to her that traditional Freudian principles of psychoanalysis were aimed at keeping patients away from the truth about their childhood. Freud himself, she discovered, had begun to perceive that parents often abuse their children. The culture in which he had been brought up, itself the creation of people who had suffered in childhood, forbade him even to entertain such an idea. So he set about building theories which could protect him from the forbidden truth.

The semi-divinity of parents

His disciples were only too willing to collaborate in this shoring up of parental semi-divinity. It satisfied their sense of what was fitting. They did not ask themselves why they had such a sense.

If they had done so they might have come to understand, as Dr. Miller did, that children do not necessarily revere their parents because the parents are selfless and heroically loving. In fact, it often happens that parents treat their helpless children in a way which makes the youngsters indignant, confused and frustrated. When they give expression to their feelings their all-powerful parents suppress them, telling them that because they are young they cannot ever be allowed to assert themselves or demand justice.

Sometimes the hurt they feel is unendurable. Since they cannot bear it, they must transform it into something which they can bear. They deny the very nature of what their parents have done to them, and insist that they, the children, deserved it. Naturally, in order to sustain this idealised picture of the adults in their life they cannot avoid investing them with a kind of divinity. Like the gods of many ancient religions parents have no obligation to explain or justify the things they do. If they hurt their children it can only be because the children have deserved it (even if they do not know how), or because the adults' superior wisdom tells them that the children's suffering will 'benefit' them in some wonderful way when they grow up.

This bleak conception of children's place in the world leaves no room for the normal human responses to being controlled or punished. Our culture requires children to behave as if they accepted their situation philosophically. If they do not, if they retaliate or even look defiant they risk being punished severely. Generally they adopt the safe option: docility, and a fundamental denial of their real feelings.

Having submitted body and soul to the adults in their lives, children are forced to forget how angry and unhappy they made them feel. They remember only the growing strength of purpose, their apparent pitilessness, their godlike indifference to unimportant people like them. These become 'good' qualities in the children's estimation and as they grow they begin to build them into their personalities. The repressed, and by now lost, memories of the pain their parents inflicted on them with these very same 'qualities' - the irony is deeply tragic - provide the motive force which impels them eventually to do to their own children what their parents did to them.

I recognise that this account of some of Dr. Miller's essential thought is infirm in many ways. I am not a psychotherapist and I have no right to suggest that I have any professional understanding of her ideas. I feel reasonably sure, however, that I have said nothing which is totally contrary to them. My purpose is not to paraphrase her books, but by describing and exploring the effect they had on my thinking, to commend them to other educators. I sincerely believe that anyone who is seriously interested in freeing society from the anti-libertarian influences which grip it at present needs to read and apply them.

The case of Adolf Hitler

Dr. Miller saw in the early life of Adolf Hitler how the treatment of children by parents, who believed themselves to be honest and God-fearing, could embitter the lives of those youngsters forever. Often, in Western Europe at least, parental oppression was buttressed by an unforgiving Old Testament version of religion. The doctrine of Original Sin authorised adults to assume that their children were bound to do wrong sooner or later, and therefore to need severe punishment. Since it was only a matter of time before a youngster went off the rails, they reasoned, a responsible parent would be vigilant and correct the first signs of naughtiness as memorably as possible. If that did not work, if children continued to show signs of waywardness, they were clearly under the powerful influence of evil and needed a double dose of chastisement.

Since the parent alone was entitled to decide what was and was not 'good behaviour', Hitler's father, Alois, possessed a uniquely tyrannical power over the young Adolf. At any time of the day or night he could deem anything the boy did to be a breach of his filial duty, and punish him for it in any way he thought proper. No-one outside the family would think, even for a moment, of defending him. His mother, Klara, could do nothing which might have undermined her lord and master's absolute immunity from criticism. With the sole limitation that he had to avoid killing his son (though even that might have been accepted if the 'provocation' had warranted it), Alois could do exactly what he wished.

Rudolf Olden, in his biography of Hitler, has a vivid picture of Hitler's father:

> "Even after he retired, he retained the typical pride of a bureaucrat and insisted upon being addressed as 'Herr' followed by his title, whereas the farmers and labourers used the informal form of address ['Du'] with one another. By showing him the

respect he demanded, the local people were really making fun of this outsider. He was never on good terms with the people he knew. To make up for it he established a nice little dictatorship in his home. His wife looked up to him and he treated his children with a hard hand. Adolf in particular he had no understanding for. He tyrannised him. If he wanted the boy to come to him, the former non-commissioned officer would whistle on two fingers."

It is as well to remember that the young Adolf, while he was living through this daily experience of brutal contempt, could not relieve his pain, as most adults can, by asserting his human right to be treated correctly. Neither could he imagine a time in the future when his age and maturity would protect him from being the helpless victim of his father's caprice. He faced a stark choice: to resent what his father was doing to him and express that resentment openly, or to accept, dutifully, that he deserved every blow he received.

It is impossible to be certain how far Hitler espoused one or other of these alternatives. He does not appear to have spoken openly against his father. In 'Mein Kampf' he calls him 'Herr Vater' (literally 'Mr Father'), and records that he had on occasion to drag him out of taverns the worse for drink, but there is no sign of a consistent, sustained attack on Alois' conduct towards his son. Such evidence as there is suggests that everyone who commented on the Fuehrer's father, including Hitler himself, spoke in conventionally respectful terms of a man who might not have been perfect, but who did a thorough and dutiful job of bringing up his children in a social tradition based on the assumed virtues of Christianity.

If Hitler had been merely an ordinary civil criminal we might not be over-concerned with his childhood. Dr. Miller, however, argues persuasively that the monster he became, the author of a genocide which will probably be linked with his name as long as humanity exists, was the natural product of Herr Vater's regime. Therefore, it may fairly be said that the millions who paid with their lives for the Fuehrer's infernal vision died at the hands of Alois Hitler as much as those of his son.

If this is true, if, as I suggested in *Compulsory Schooling Disease,* Hitler was not a cancerous growth on the otherwise healthy body of humanity, but rather a normal product of European child-rearing who found himself in a position to mobilise millions of others like him - it seems at least possible to argue that the cause of war, and of the social phenomena which resemble it, is the unrecognised abuse of children by their parents.

To say this without qualification is, I recognise, to risk the scorn of most social commentators and historians. They would, I imagine, reject the idea that any single influence could generate the complex of upheavals and antagonisms which characterise war. They would insist that nationalism, racial tension, religious differences and the like were to blame for most outbreaks of hostility, and that if a solution to them existed it was to be found in negotiation between diplomats and statesmen.

A source of hate and oppression

I am in no position to argue with them. I learned a lot from Dr. Miller's books about the reasons why people so often hate and oppress each other, but I also came to realise that the social legislators, the educationists and media pundits, the very ones who might have taken her ideas and used them to advantage had themselves all been children. The truth which could have illuminated their study of society and enabled them to understand where racism and nationalism come from was hidden by the repressed pain which they had suffered when they were children, and which they had been forced to forget.

In that forgetting lies, I believe, the key which unlocks the secret not only of individual anguish and violence, but also of the pervasive oppression underlying the structure of society. To understand better how this deep but unrecognised tide of suffering shows itself, we must look at attitudes which have become part of the fabric of society to such an extent that we find ourselves recoiling instinctively from any critique of them, almost as if they were sacred. Indeed, they are sacred, at least to the extent that they express a metaphysical perception, a response to things greater and more terrible than ordinary language can express.

Such an examination is dangerous. I have noticed that whenever I suggest that there may be a connection between what happens to people when they are children and their behaviour as adults the atmosphere cools. I begin to feel that I have trespassed upon ground which is fenced in with invisible barriers which I am expected to recognise and required to respect.

Honour thy monstrous father

Dr. Miller illustrates the strength of these barriers when she recounts, in *Banished Knowledge: Facing childhood injuries* how the son of Hans Frank, the Nazi governor of Poland, who was responsible for appalling acts of genocide and oppression, condemned his father for his war crimes. He had nothing to say by way of mitigation. In a interview for 'Stern' in 1987 he spoke simply, with clarity and detachment, as a representative of the human race and an embodiment of its better aspirations, about the unforgivable things his father had done. He repudiated them and the man who was responsible for them, without reservation or special pleading.

A storm of anger broke over him. The press was full of letters from 'decent German citizens' who thought that, hideous though Frank's crimes had been, the worst of them was that he had produced such a son. Others might be within their rights to condemn the infamous things the father had done, they said, but a son must realise that as far as his father's unspeakable actions were concerned he could not be a normal human being. His filial duty forbade him to be angry on behalf of the people his father had killed. He had to honour a man who had no right to be honoured, because that man was his father. That obligation was absolute and supreme.

I do not think that the people who condemned the son were themselves all Nazis or necessarily sympathetic to oppression. They might have been, of course: the old canker of fascism is still alive and virulent in Europe. Nonetheless, I tend to think that the openness of their reaction suggests rather that they honestly felt that the bond between a father and his son sweeps aside even the most pressing moral imperatives.

I draw from this the conclusion that early childhood experiences create for most people a moral map in which the character and purposes of their parents lie at the centre, shaping and defining every other belief and sentiment they may have. As often happens where the human psyche is concerned pain leaves a deeper mark than pleasure. The need to make sense of hurtful experiences concentrates the resources of a small child's soul and from the struggle, which ensues between his feeble, unformed individuality and the vast, incomparably more powerful universe which enfolds him, emerges a distorted, unbalanced understanding of what it is to be human.

Perhaps an incident from my own early life will illustrate the tragic depth of childhood trauma. When I was a toddler, I lived with my mother in South London. My father was absent much of the time in the Forces and my mother had to look after me alone in a rented house. I have never had to care for a child who could not talk properly and be reasoned with, so I cannot imagine how my being such a child made problems for her. Probably I annoyed her from time to time by doing things which disturbed her. Like any normal person, she probably wanted very much to reason with me, to use the civilised weapons of persuasion and entreaty to bring me under control.

Unfortunately, small children, even when they have begun to understand their mother tongue, often do not grasp that the words: "Do not do that or I will punish you", are a real, serious warning of what will happen if they continue to do what they are doing. They have not yet forged the link between the nominal meaning of words and the complex series of actions which that meaning conveys to an adult.

One day I was drawing on some paper with a stub of blue pencil. I was enjoying myself, experimenting with shapes, trying to make my hands do what the grown-ups seemed to be able to manage easily. Inevitably, the blue lines wandered from the paper onto the wall, and I was in trouble. My mother told me that if I did it again she would throw my pencil in the fire, which happened to be burning in the room where we were. The words came into my consciousness not as a threat but as an absurdity. The rules of life as I construed them at the time did not include such a sequence of events. I had already discovered that people I loved and trusted sometimes hit me, but that was part of the continuum of touches and handlings, from hugs and kisses to blows, with which I was familiar. I was learning how to handle it. This threat was different. I could not visualise, or in any other way experiment with the idea that my pencil could be wrenched out of my hand and burnt.

Inevitably I drew on the wall again, and my pencil went into the fire. The floor gave way under me and angled itself madly down into darkness. A voice which must have been mine but which I could not control or understand howled in my ears. I fell into the void which only I could see, reaching out with my small hands towards solidities which were supposed to be there, but weren't. The world no longer worked and I could not bear to live in it, yet I had no choice but to go on. I watched the pencil burn. The flames took it from me, and perhaps for the first time in my life I experienced finality. I could only scream.

I imagine my mother thought, as people of her generation often did, that I was 'manipulating' her, playing on her emotions as if I were an adult and knew how to simulate feelings I did not really have. I do not remember if she tried to stop me or frighten me into silence. I could not have stopped, whatever she did.

The suffering of children

I do not tell this story because it illustrates Dr. Miller's thesis. I remember the incident, so it is unlikely to have burrowed down into my subconscious mind and engendered neuroses. I only recount it because it shows how easily events which adults see as trivial hurt children terribly. Adults cannot enter into the suffering of their children and recognise that it is sharpened by the very limitations which make young peoples' concerns appear trivial when seen from the outside. Even if they could, they have learned from a tradition which has soaked into our culture that paying attention to children when they show signs of distress or frustration is irresponsible. It might 'spoil' them, or give them an ascendancy over their parents.

We have painted for ourselves a picture of childhood which makes this sort of thinking seem natural. We believe that children pass their time in a cloud of golden-tinted innocence marred only by occasional bouts of 'naughtiness'. We assume that if their emotions are stirred up it is only for short time, and they soon forget whatever has worried them. A cliché which I often hear in discussions about what is wrong with our young people holds that 'children aren't allowed to be children these days'. This suggests that by letting children share something of the life they will have as adults we stop them appreciating the bliss which is popularly supposed to come from ignorance.

If adults looked back into their own recollections they might find a radically different truth. They might remember, as I do, resenting the fact that their parents and the rest of the grown-up world thought of them almost entirely in terms of what they could not do. Perhaps they would also remember the times when they tried to seize control of some part of their life before their parents considered they were ready to do so, and were crushed.

Unfortunately, this clear perception of the past rarely happens. More often than not, peoples' early experiences of pain and frustration, repressed and then transformed by the subtle working of the subconscious, caused them to identify with their own parents, the very ones who oppressed them. They pattern their behaviour on the more or less tyrannical power-plays which they had to submit to when they were young. As a result the cycle continues and the corrosive, hate-engendering cancer of parental abuse goes on.

Private suffering and private consequences

The reader may be asking at this point how all this relates to society in general. We may well agree that abusive parenting tends to create problems for individual families: it may even be a significant factor in the genesis of crime. But to argue from individual tragedies to psychotic outbreaks on a national scale, such as the Hitler regime in Germany, might seem irresponsible even to a person who was sympathetic to some aspects of Alice Miller's thinking.

In a later chapter, I shall comment on the prevalence of covertness and dishonesty in the organisation of modern society. I believe that the campaign against truth and honesty which is waged at every level of society by whoever happens to be in a position of power reflects macrocosmically the way in which most children are forced to deny the vehemence of their own feelings and behave as if they were happy when they are not. At this point I wish only to suggest that insofar as Society is organised by adults it is possible that their actions, and their motives, are not necessarily what they claim them to be.

Our penal system furnishes many examples of this fundamental dishonesty. We know that prison is by far the least effective way of punishing delinquents. It tends to harden criminals and confirm them in their offending ways. I suspect that because it hurts and demeans them without bringing them to an intelligent understanding of why their behaviour cannot be tolerated it operates as a kind of latter-day slavery. After all, slavery is the oppression of innocent men and women, and until they face and courageously denounce their own wrong-doing, that is exactly what prisoners believe themselves to be.

Instead of demonstrating to criminals how we want them to behave towards the rest of Society by treating the roots of their offending, we tend to look for ways to make their lives more uncomfortable. There is a strong current of opinion in

Society which holds that we can best deal with prisoners by deterring them. Penologists, who mostly agree that such a policy only embitters criminals and intensifies their anti-social attitudes, are denounced as 'bleeding-heart liberals' or some similar opprobrious label. Periodically, Home Secretaries of all parties strengthen their credit with the public by declaring that criminality is nothing to do with background, upbringing or economic circumstances, and everything to do with simple wickedness and the decline of old-fashioned severity.

This irrational resistance to the plain, demonstrable truth, this radical preference for a retrograde system of thought, which consistently produces more crime rather than less, must have its origins in the enforced concealment of childhood pain. The criminal receives the full weight of the anger and frustration which so many voters, judges, politicians and prison officers endured in silence when they were young. The child in them cannot countenance, even for a moment, showing mercy to his oppressor.

The inevitable result of this inability to see and tackle the forces from which our angry, vengeful feelings come, is that a leaden weight is attached to every movement towards a happier, more liberal and kinder society. Even people who sincerely want to free society from the gross cruelties which disfigure it find that they have to pay passing honours to the retributive lobby, the punishers and the moralisers. So crime increases, more money is spent uselessly on repressing it, and the resources which might have procured a genuine change in the attitudes of criminals are dispersed and wasted.

By recoiling from a humane and positive approach to offenders we actually spend our money on a proven means of generating more crime: the old, punitive, squalid, corrosive prison system. We cannot seriously aim at eliminating cruelty and oppression from our society until we confront the truth about its origins, and most important of all, cease the self-deception which allows us to call the abuse of our fellow human beings - whatever their age - morality and common-sense.

Chapter two

Poisoned relationships

Every ruler, and every person whose position allows him to behave like a ruler, tends to treat his subjects as he was himself treated when he was a child. Whenever a person finds himself empowered to make decisions which others have to accept and obey, he draws on the mental constructs stored in his mind by the interaction of his childhood emotions with his parents' commanding, manipulative power.

I can sympathise with any reader who finds such a formulation implausible. Our culture has taught us that adults are independent-minded people who always make serious, mature decisions, whereas children tend to act on impulse, moved by whim or by a desire to usurp grown-up prerogatives before they can be trusted with them. To suggest that adult emotions develop from those of children seems subversive, not to say wilfully unreasonable. Yet the lives of Hitler and his fellow tyrants Stalin and Nicolae Ceausescu, under Dr. Miller's analysis, reveal a consistent pattern of brutalisation in childhood. It would surely be perverse to suggest that the manifest horror they presided over when they grew up had nothing to do with that ill-treatment.

All three of them were raised by fathers who beat them without mercy and denied them the comfort of emotional warmth when they were almost unimaginably vulnerable. In all of their adult lives we can perceive a symbolic re-enactment of the transactions between father and son.

Just as the young Hitler lived with the knowledge that he could be beaten at any moment as hard and as long as Alois saw fit, so he created in Germany a 'household' in which Jews could be beaten at any time, without any reason other than that they were members of a race which it had been traditional to regard as 'outsiders'.

The target of Stalin's anger was not even a specific race. He oppressed his people at random, sending out orders to his regional surrogates to round up fixed quotas of 'enemies of the People' and deliver them to the Gulag like so many wagon-loads of potatoes. There is no need to emphasise that they were entirely innocent of any crime: the fact is well known. Their tragedy was simply that they were available when the moment came for Stalin's suppressed rage against his parents to be worked out on somebody.

Nicolae Ceausescu's father was an alcoholic who spent what little money he had on drink. As a result his family often had to go without food for long stretches of time. He beat his children daily both because he was drunk and because it was 'for their own good' - the catch-all justification for parental brutality almost since humanity began.

At first, the young Nicolae could find relief for the repressed rage his father had condemned him to carry within him only by killing young animals. Later, when he had grown up and could begin to give maturer expression to the darkness in his soul, he discovered the Communist Party. It gave him the ladder he needed to reach a position from which he could take revenge on his heartless father. Tragically, the victim of his dammed-up anger was not the drink-swilling peasant who had oppressed him. He was dead by then. The people of Romania stood in for him and paid the price for his cruelty.

The corps of auxiliary tyrants

Dr. Miller points out that none of these mass murderers acted alone. Without the active collaboration of police, local government officials, army officers, teachers and administrators, Hitler could never have enslaved the German people. Shorn of the vast network of secret policemen, torturers and informers who believed that the highest form of duty was to carry out his orders, Stalin would have been powerless. He would have gone down in history as nothing more than a neurotic, wild-eyed ex-seminarian. However hideous his private vision of society it would have remained locked in his tormented brain. The world might have been spared a massacre of mythic proportions if there had not been a corps of auxiliaries who thought like him.

I believe that too little attention has been paid by historians and social scientists to the mentality of these obedient little people, the gauleiters, the Gestapo, the

Chekists and the Securitate. History records what they did but rarely asks why they did it. The moral cleaning-up process which happens when oppressive regimes fall apart generally operates on the principle that the servants of the tyrant are simply evil people who seized their chance to satisfy their base instincts. The acts of the people who organise the terror and plan the social upheaval associated with totalitarian governments are usually presented as unaccountable, obscene departures from normal humanity, the appalling result of cynical choices. Their judges usually claim, as the Allies did at Nuremburg, that they are trying them and punishing them in the name of normal, decent humanity.

This interpretation is seductive. It allows us to isolate the extreme cruelty of a man like Adolf Eichmann, for example, from tendencies which undoubtedly exist in the general population, and to pronounce upon it as if we had nothing in common with it. I believe, however, the truth is very different.

Adolf Eichmann

Eichmann's cold-eyed cruelty appears exceptional and bizarre because it operated on an epic scale. We see him as a monster whose vileness sets him apart from ordinary Germans because he arranged, single-handed, the transport of millions of people to their deaths. We are fascinated by the bureaucratic banality of his crime. We are amazed to learn that he went to great trouble to negotiate with the Reichsbahn concessionary party tickets for the martyred Jews who were notionally his 'clients', so that his office would not have to pay so much for their transport. His cruelty transcended even the great pogroms of earlier centuries in being dispassionate. The Crusaders and the Cossacks killed Jews because they hated them for being, as they saw it, a different kind of human being. Eichmann transported the Jews to death because he thought of them as goods, or as cattle, who happened to look like human beings. Yet when we look at his childhood we see influences common to many, perhaps most young Germans of his time, which may have made him what he was.

The man who captured him in Argentina and brought him back to Israel records this about Eichmann:

> *"Eichmann was born in Solingen, Germany, the first of five children. When he was eight, his accountant father moved the*

> *family to Linz, Austria, to become a commercial manager at the*
> *electric works. A remote figure, stern and deeply devout, for*
> *many years an honorary elder of the town's Evangelical*
> *congregation, Karl Eichmann ran an austere and loveless*
> *household. Above all else, it nurtured respect for thrift and*
> *order."*
> (***Eichmann In My Hands***, Peter Malkin & Harry Stein, 1990, Muller.)

How much pain is compressed into those few words it is hard to tell. For an active, enquiring child the sort of treatment by which an 'austere and loveless' household nurtured 'respect for thrift and order' must have been almost unendurable. In fact, Peter Malkin, who captured him, records that he was 'uncertain and withdrawn' as a youngster, and we may surmise that he had learned very early in his life that it was extremely unsafe to question his father or differ from him.

Later, Eichmann joined the SS, based outside Dachau in Southern Germany. The training he had to undergo was brutal, but he thrived on it. He was made to crawl over barbed wire, and ever afterwards, when he showed off the wounds in his elbows and knees, he boasted that he had rid himself of all susceptibility to pain. No doubt his father's 'discipline' had given him every opportunity to learn how to suppress hurt feelings and feign acceptance of the unacceptable.

When the Israeli Secret Service tracked him down in Argentina and took him into their custody, he revealed how completely he had surrendered any normal instincts he might have had under the determining influence of his appalling childhood. Kidnapped and hidden in a safe house, Eichmann made no attempt to escape, or to resist the Israeli agents who interrogated him. He had assimilated them in his mind into the relational construct of which his father was the archetypal head. They were not Jews: they were Authority.

As he answered their questions, with care and every appearance of respect, he showed them that at no point did their moral world connect with his:

> ' *"Es war den Auftrag den ich hatte,"* he said evenly. *"Ich hatte*
> *den Auftrag zu erfullen."* (It was a job I had. I had a job to do.)

> *"Just a job?"*

He hesitated, perhaps surprised by the vehemence of the reaction. "You must believe me, it wasn't something I planned, nor anything I'd have chosen."

......Working from within, he had always argued for moderation. But he was a soldier - in this he took enormous pride and a soldier is never entirely his own man. When decisions were made by those above, and orders issued, they had to be obeyed. This was duty. For him, this was a matter of moral responsibility.

Listening, it was not quite so easy as I had supposed to frame cogent replies. I had imagined he would be defensive, that he would express at least token remorse. Instead he talked as if he had spent those years working as a grocery clerk.

......When he finished I made no reply.

"You must believe me," he added suddenly. "I had nothing against the Jews." '

At another point in the interrogation Eichmann spoke of his love for children.

' "Ich liebe Kinder (I love children)," he put it to me one night early on, smiling almost dreamily.

"Sie lieben Kinder?" I shot back, unable to help myself. "You must mean some children."

"Nein, ich liebe alle Kinder (I love all children)."

"Do you?" Once again, I found myself struggling for self-control in his presence." '

Eichmann stoutly denied the accusation that he was an antisemite.

' "In fact", he continued, "Ich war den Juden immer zugeneigt (I had always been fond of Jews). I had Jewish friends. When I was

*touring Haifa, I made a point of finding Jewish taxi-drivers. I
always liked the Jews better than the Arabs." '*

*Eichmann had even gone so far as to learn some Hebrew.
'.....Something had occurred to him. "I do remember one
prayer....." And tilting back his head, he began to intone:"Shma
yisrael, adonai elohenu, adonai echad."*

*The most sacred prayer of our people, the death-bed profession of
faith of every pious Jew:"Hear, O Israel, the Lord our God, the
Lord is One."*

*I felt myself beginning to shake with rage. "Eichmann, do you
have any idea of the meaning of these words?"*

*"Ja," he replied genially, and proceeded to offer an accurate
translation in German.*

*"Perhaps you're familiar with some other words," I said. "Aba.
Ima. Do those ring a bell?"*

*"Aba, Ima," he mused, trying to recall. "I don't really remember.
What do they mean?"*

*"Daddy, Mommy. It's what Jewish children scream when they are
torn from their parents' arms." I paused, almost unable to contain
myself. "My sister's boy, my favourite playmate, he was just your
son's age. Also blond and blue-eyed, just like your son. And you
killed him."*

*Genuinely perplexed by the observation, he actually waited a
moment to see if I would clarify it. "Yes," he said finally, "but he
was Jewish, wasn't he?" '*

Moral deadness of this order is almost impossible to comment on without a
mixture of passion and horror. Reading words like these ought to establish us
permanently in a new universe of discourse where all easy talk about discipline
and duty becomes impossible. Unfortunately, we have learned to believe that

there is no kinship between what Eichmann did and anything which happens in the workaday world.

The 'little' Eichmanns

Yet throughout Germany millions of other little Eichmanns were at work at the same time, lubricating with their meticulous pen-pushing and file-card shuffling the soulless engine which was grinding European Jewry to death. I surmise that many of them, perhaps a preponderant majority, shared Eichmann's worldview, in broad outline, at least.

Not all of them, it is true, had the opportunity which fate allotted to Eichmann, to preside over mass killings and congratulate themselves on the efficiency and bureaucratic polish of their execution. Yet few of them possessed the moral courage to refuse their co-operation. Like Eichmann himself, they may claim to have had their doubts about the precise working out of the Final Solution, but their choice to become guards, administrators, secret policemen and the like clearly shows that they were blind to an elementary moral truth. They could not see that there is not, and never will be, a proper way, a justified, moral way, to wipe out a people.

Why were so many ordinary, unexceptional little men and women prepared to kill their neighbour? Did the Devil afflict them with moral insanity, or did they decide in an act of collective cynicism to say "Evil be thou my good"? We can be sure of one thing: Hitler's mind-set harmonised well with that of his followers and of the German people as a community. He did not have to overcome inbred resistance to the idea of genocide. He found a people ready and willing to treat with contempt anyone he considered less worthy. He also found a community which already possessed a collective image of the kind of person who 'deserved' to be treated in such a way. That person was a child.

Bruno Bettelheim, who spent time in Dachau before the War, records how prisoners learned to behave like half-wits, clumsily tripping over their feet or dropping things like uncoordinated toddlers. He records how the guards behaved as if it was their duty to 'educate' their prisoners (many of whom were, in fact, senior academics and professional people of the highest possible culture) by 'supervising' their washing and even their visits to the lavatory. The message they seemed to be giving the inmates was that they were in the camp partly because, like children, they needed 'training' in the simplest aspects of civilised living.

When they were not killing the prisoners for sport, the guards often adopted towards them the role, familiar to anyone who has observed ordinary adults with their children, of harsh parents, exasperated beyond belief by the wilful obstructiveness of their young. Often they would set the prisoners demeaning tasks to perform. Naturally, the prisoners often failed to perform them 'adequately' and had to be punished. The punishment generally involved a beating, inflicted on the prisoner's buttocks, after he had let down his own trousers. It is worth noting that children are frequently punished in the same way: spanking or caning on the backside is felt in many European cultures to be especially appropriate for immature people, as an alternative to whipping on the back, a man's punishment.

It is impossible to determine exactly how far the guards' behaviour expressed a conscious plan of action. Just as Eichmann was able to separate in his mind 'all children', whom he loved, and 'Jewish children', whom he had orders to kill, it is possible that some, at least, of the men who staffed the concentration camps had lost any sense that the prisoners were human beings, individuals with names, professions, family trees, and kinship with those who oppressed them. Their relationships with the human cattle they were paid to contain may well have been delineated by the mythic image embodied in the latter's utter weakness, their unimaginable vulnerability.

I suspect that all totalistic institutions (even relatively benign ones like schools) make their inhabitants, both staff and inmates, treat each other in certain common and predictable ways, as they fit their behaviour into the relational structure imposed by their environment. It seems reasonable to suppose that just as the prisoners' conduct was influenced by the constraints they had to live under so the guards played the role suggested by their absolute ascendancy.

What is the relevance of all this to post-war, post-Holocaust society? Have we anything in common with the monsters who did European Jewry to death?

The fascist tendency in modern society

I want to suggest that all the ways of thought from which the Holocaust came are present now in our supposedly settled, civilised world. I believe that we ordinary, 'good' people are subject to the very same forces that formed the Nazi criminals. By the same token, I suspect that the institutions by which we mould citizens when they are young and corral them when they become inconvenient are only different from the concentration camps in that the destructive forces latent in them have not found an outlet through which they can amplify themselves into mass-murder.

Restraints of law and custom derived from a long experience of relative economic and social stability operate in a country like ours to absorb much of the repressed tension and grief people bring with them into adult life. As a result we have been spared the sight of storm-troopers in our streets, beating up our fellow-citizens and drawing us into a nightmare world of lies made truth by means of torture and persecution. Instead we have grown up with an array of customary attitudes which, while they do no physical harm to anyone, poison and degrade the relationships people in our Society assume they must have with those around them.

People do not generally work out the bitterness of their childhood with machine-guns and poison gas. That tends to happen only when political tension and social unrest have weakened the moral veto which holds genocidal impulses in check. Instead, their repressed anguish finds expression in social attitudes tinged with a pervasive authoritarianism, a disposition to want ascendancy over others.

They feel offended by libertarian ideas and by demands for greater tolerance. The thought that criminals might, instead of being punished, receive treatment designed to change their mind-set fills them with anger. They are to be seen at party conferences cheering to the echo every promise from Ministers to make life harder for under-groups like single parents and immigrants.

The people who express these feelings never reflect on the reasons why they have them. They assume that they are 'common-sense' and natural. They tell each other that only 'loony-Left', politically-motivated elements in Society disagree with them. If they hear of liberal initiatives in education or social work they berate the authors of them as 'do-gooders', instinctively acknowledging by that choice of words that doing good has no place in the programme of social control patterned in them by their treatment when they were children. They are convinced that human society will always be regulated by suspicion and harshness.

The poison injected into their lives when as small children they faced the impossibility of resisting their parents' godlike manipulation distorts and sours their adult lives. It creates in the personality of many normal people a subtle craving to put others in chains, to revive in the lives of their fellows the bitterness of their own childhood.

The 'Poisonous Pedagogy'

In her book *For Your Own Good*, Alice Miller devotes much analysis to this mechanism. She attributes to it not only the ferocity of the Nazis but also the microcosmic tyranny of abusive parents and teachers. As she says (p168)

> "...teachers are only too happy to take over for the father when it comes to disciplining the pupil and ... they have much to gain from it in the way of their own narcissistic stabilisation."

Dr. Miller examines the impact of abusive parenting on the way in which people respond to the experience of school. She notes that Hitler began to do poorly at school about the time when his father almost beat him to death for trying to run away from the family home. She suggests that he had internalised Alois and could not feel directly the principled human indignation which might have afforded him a measure of relief from his anguish if he had been able to express it. Instead he resorted to the only weapon he could use to punish his father, in the symbolic person of his teacher - poor work, ill-executed and more or less imperfectly learned.

Hitler's rejection of schooling and all it stood for went much further when he achieved his apotheosis as Fuehrer. He ordered the burning of books by freethinking authors, and the proscription of artists whose work in any way expressed a sensibility at variance with his own. I have seen many times a film taken at a Nazi rally at which hundreds of people, compatriots of Goethe, Schiller, Mozart, Beethoven, Thomas Mann and countless other giants, circled a vast pyre and threw onto it thousands of books, exulting in the illusion of purity and purgation created by the leaping flames against the darkness.

Only when I read Dr. Miller's books, however, did I sense the psychological authenticity of the ceremony. These things cannot easily be done by day. Darkness pictures for those who feel the need to burn books many aspects of their tormented lives - despair, rage, confusion, and the limitless fear of the beaten child. To dispel that gloom with a fire nourished by books, the basic tools of formal education, compounds the tragedy with a stratum of almost unbearable irony. Instead of freeing them from anguish the flames conspired with the darkness to obliterate their individuality. It turned them into demonic ciphers intent on creating in a tangible form the Hell which was inside them, where they struggled eternally against the images of all those who had made them and their forebears suffer.

The way out of this manifest horror is not easy to chart. Its causes are dyed into the fabric of our supposedly developed society. Yet Dr. Miller met at least one person who was in no danger of succumbing to it. He was an old man. He sat down next to her on a park bench. She noticed that he spoke in an attentive, respectful way to some children who were playing nearby, and she struck up a conversation with him. She learned that he had been a soldier in the Great War. He said that he felt as if he had lived a charmed life: many of his friends had been killed, but he had survived without a scratch. He seemed to have a complete trust in a benevolent fate:

> *"Thus when I asked about his siblings, it didn't surprise me to hear him answer: "They are all dead; I was my mother's pet." His mother "loved life," he said. Sometimes in the spring she would wake him up in the morning to go with her and listen to the birds singing in the woods before he went to school. These were his happiest memories. When I asked whether he had been given beatings, he answered:"Hardly ever; my father's hand may have slipped occasionally. That made me angry every time, but he never did it in my mother's presence; she would never have permitted it. But you know," he went on, "once I was beaten by my teacher. In the first three grades I was the best pupil, then in the fourth we got a new teacher. One time he accused me of something I hadn't done. Then he took me aside and started*

hitting me and kept on hitting, shouting like a madman the whole time, 'Now will you tell the truth?' But how could I? After all, I would have had to lie to satisfy him, and I had never done that before because I had no reason to be afraid of my parents. So I endured the beating for a quarter of an hour, but I never cared for school after that, and became a poor pupil. It often distressed me later that I never got my high-school diploma. But I don't think I had any choice at the time."

"As a child this man appeared to have been held in such esteem by his mother that he in turn was able to respect and express his feelings. He was therefore AWARE of being angry with his father when the latter's 'hand slipped'; he was AWARE that his teacher was forcing him to tell a lie and demeaning him, and he also felt grief because he had to pay for his integrity by neglecting his education because there was no other way for him at the time. I noticed that he didn't say, like most people, "My mother loved me very much," but instead, "She loved life," and I recalled having once written that about Goethe's mother. This elderly man had known his happiest moments in the woods with his mother when he had sensed her delight in the birds and shared it with her. Their warm relationship still shone in his ageing eyes, and her regard for him expressed itself unmistakably in the way he now was speaking to the children at play."

(***For Your Own Good***, page 169)

The respect we accord to our children, our readiness to share with them the unique joy which comes from being alive, and above all our determination to root out from our own lives the residue of pain which we thoughtlessly inflict on them will determine how far our society progresses in the next century. A great deal remains to be done, but few parents and even fewer educators seem to have understood the breadth and depth of the task.

Chapter three

Unkind education makes unkind institutions

When I began to teach, more than 30 years ago, I set out to be a fierce disciplinarian. I was a Grammar School usher at the time, scarcely more than a schoolboy myself and determined to succeed at my first job. I stalked about the place, giving orders and behaving as I thought teachers were supposed to behave. I was long on formality and short on humour; I probably bored the boys witless, but by and large I felt I had them in hand.

At the time I thought no more about the situation than that I was doing what was expected of me and justifying my salary. If I had been able to look into the future and draw into my thinking some of the ideas I was to meet when I was an experienced teacher, I might have been invaded by doubts about the fundamental value of the authority-games I was playing. I might have realised that I was taking part in a centuries-old process described by Alice Miller as follows:

> *"The individual psychological stages in the lives of most people are:*
>
> *1. To be hurt as a small child without anyone recognising the situation as such.*
>
> *2. To fail to react to the resulting suffering with anger.*
>
> *3. To show gratitude for what are supposed to be good intentions* (on the part of one's parents and educators - C.S).
>
> *4. To forget everything.*

5. To discharge the stored-up anger onto others in adulthood, or to direct it against oneself."
(**For Your Own Good** page 106)

I realise now that my heavy-handed control (which included, to my shame, the formal, authorised beating of boys when their behaviour offended me), was nothing more than accumulated anger. As I transformed my classroom into a microcosm of the State, which is itself a magnified projection of the Family, I had allowed the bitterness of my own childhood to imprint itself on my every word and gesture.

Like every young teacher I had been told that it was fatal to unbend, to speak to the children with warmth or humour, as if I liked them and enjoyed their company. It worries me now that I found this 'wisdom' easy to accept, because I am not by nature a cold person, but at the time I became good at it. I punished pupils without much compunction, and I was delighted to hear, on the 'grape-vine', that among the boys I passed for a 'strict' teacher. By common agreement on both sides of the Staff-room door 'strict' meant the same as 'good'.

Yet as I look back on those times, I am forced to confront the sheer inhumanity of my behaviour. It amazes me that I, and every other teacher in that school, thought responsible education necessarily entailed deliberately frightening children and talking to them as if they were both stupid and evil. I now know what animates the 'Theatre of Anger' which I and so many of my colleagues played out in our classrooms, but I am still horrified to think that we educators, for all our professional acumen, could not perceive the damage we were certainly doing to the pupils. We all knew our subjects, but we knew nothing about the most important part of education, the creation of an emotional structure which will enable the pupil to live a self-confident, un-neurotic life.

The unkind secondary school

As a secondary teacher, I took charge of pupils during the storms of puberty. Alice Miller describes this time and the dramas it produces thus:

"Parents (and, I believe, teachers, as parent-surrogates - C.S.) *often have such success with the numerous methods they use to*

subdue their children that they don't encounter any problems until the children reach puberty........The parents cannot understand the sudden change; they are left helpless and uncomprehending by an adolescent who seems to be rejecting all norms and whose self-destructive behaviour cannot be modified by logical arguments or by the subtle devices of 'poisonous pedagogy.

At puberty adolescents are often taken totally by surprise by the intensity of their true feelings, after having succeeded in keeping them at a distance during the latency period. With the spurt of biological growth, these feelings (rage, anger, rebelliousness, falling in love, sexual desire, enthusiasm, joy, enchantment, sadness) seek full expression, but in many cases this would endanger the parents' (and by the same token, the teacher's - C.S.) *psychic balance. If adolescents were to show their true feelings openly they would run the risk of being sent to prison as dangerous terrorists or put in mental institutions as insane. Our society would no doubt have nothing but a psychiatric clinic to offer Shakespeare's Hamlet or Goethe's Werther, and Schiller's Karl Moor would probably have the same fate."* (ibid. Page 107)

Because I was an actor in the drama of my pupils' adolescence, I could not take the essential backward step which would have carried me to a place where I could look objectively at my pupils' feelings, and respect them as they deserved to be respected. Instead I did what every generation of schoolmasters has done since schools began: I treated my boys' explosive, tempestuous feelings as pure, uncomplicated naughtiness. I assumed they knew their growling mulishness was 'wrong', so I felt entitled to punish them for it in any way I liked. After all, if anyone represented decent, conventional values, I did. If anyone had pointed out that adolescents often behave as they do because of emotions which lie entirely beyond their control I should have replied that they would have to get a grip on their feelings some day, and then was as good a time as any. In the simplest possible terms, I think now that I and every one of my colleagues was completely blind to our pupils' real needs, and that in consequence our work with them was an educational failure.

I will go further: all schooling which does not respectfully allow the rising generation to express painful, disturbing emotions, including those which stem from the way adults treat them, is not 'responsible' or 'disciplined'. It is unforgivably misconceived and dangerous. It creates the unwanted behaviours it piously claims to be suppressing. As Alice Miller has shown, the pain of rejection and frustrated rage which so many children feel does not go away. It doesn't fade into the common background of their everyday, insignificant feelings. It becomes the hidden dynamic of all that is most oppressive and cruel in their character. It may make them no more than harsh parents, or it may, if the right conditions prevail, enable one of them to become the embodiment of cruel patriarchy, a conscienceless dictator driven by the mad vision of a 'perfect' national family with himself as the pitiless father.

My reading of Alice Miller's books has driven me to the conclusion that the canker I have been describing extends well beyond the limits of home and school. Factories, churches, prisons, even sports teams can be theatres in which the drama of unhappy childhood is played out.

A modern hospital: an ancient oppression

It is as if the experience of being mishandled when young generates in a person's unconscious mind an infinitely adaptable 'template', formed from the dammed-up indignation of the abused child, which moulds the course of relationships in every area of life. Children who suffered in silence the ceaseless thwarting of their need for warmth and attentiveness from their parents - a substantial number if anecdotal evidence can be trusted - tend to frame their own attitudes to those around them under the shadow of that neglect.

I became aware of the working-out of this mechanism long before I had the opportunity to find out the reason for it. I had to spend a short time in hospital, for the first time since my childhood. I didn't know much about the atmosphere in a modern hospital, and I was unsure what I could expect to happen to me when I put myself into the care of the nurse and doctors.

I imagined that as an adult I could speak to the professionals as an equal partner in the process of curing my disease. I was wrong. I was back in the nursery, a child with no choices to make, no voice and no influence over my life.

It began, I think, with the thorny issue of Crossed Legs. For some reason, which no-one thought it necessary to explain to me, patients were not allowed to place one leg over the other whilst lying on their beds. There may have been some medical reason for this bizarre prohibition. Observing it might even have improved our health in some way (though I doubt it), but as far as my medically untutored eye could see it served no purpose in my hospital ward other than to furnish the nurses which a reliable motive for talking to us as if we were naughty children. The tones in which they berated us for crossing our ankles, something which normal people do without thinking when they have been lying down for some time, recalled to me vividly the robust, condescending voice of every adult who ever discovered me doing something which I ought to have known not to do.

I observed in myself, and in the other patients in the room, mainly retired men with cardiac problems, a spontaneous desire to fight back. We made a point of crossing our ankles whenever the opportunity arose to do so undetected.

The resistance movement soon expanded its campaign to include a Second Front. The ward sister had issued a decree that Tea Was Not To Be Made after a certain time. Therefore I and another patient, a retired toolmaker whom no-one would have expected to Buck the System, would trickle, all unseen. into the hot drinks kitchen to make tea at midnight. We didn't want it, but the dynamic of the situation induced in us feelings we assumed we had forgotten, and we did what children do. Fortunately we were not caught, for there was no knowing what sanctions might have been handed down to us. The punitive possibilities of a hospital do not bear too much contemplation.

Lest I be accused of building a serious case on trivial foundations I should say that these examples are important not for their detail but for the message they convey. Hospitals are naturally places where unpleasant things are often done to people who would rather not be in them. Patients understand this, and accept it in order to be cured. Their first response to being in a ward is often stoical but positive. There is no extrinsic reason for the kind of hassling and rule-making I have described. If rules have to be made it is perfectly possible to explain them to patients politely, and secure their consent to them. I and my fellow-patients were treated like children because in the minds of the people who ran the hospital that was what we were.

I believe that I suffered a re-enactment of the nurses' collective, culturally determined experience of childhood. When they rebuked me and my fellow patients for crossing our legs, not getting out of bed at the right time, and so forth, I suspect I was hearing the voice of their own parents, constantly reminding them of their subjection, their duty to obey and not to ask for explanations.

Many parents see it as their duty to teach children that they must not get in the way of what grown-ups are doing. Other adults can be reasoned with: they can have things spelled out to them and they can be expected to fit in with arrangements which have been made for their benefit. Children are different. Unless their parents come down heavily on them they are certain to mess things up. So it is wise to remind them often of their place at the bottom of the power-structure. That is what I think the nurses were doing, all unconsciously, to us. Like errant children we had to learn to accept being organised, and they were the ones to teach us.

If this were the only manifestation of this effect of repression on the everyday lives of ordinary people we could probably put up with it and think about more important things. Unfortunately the same pattern of attitudes and relationships recurs in many other places.

Sweatshops and concentration camps

Some years ago, in a small photographic development works in London, the workers, many of them women from the Indian subcontinent, decided to strike. They were used to low wages and poor conditions of service. Life has always been hard for immigrants, and doubly hard for immigrant women, but working at Grunwick had taken them into a new dimension of hardship. Ironically, the founder of the company, George Ward, was himself an Anglo-Indian, but he had forgotten, if he ever knew, the tale of injustices done by the British to the Indians. He had employed some English managers who believed it was their duty to get as much work as possible out of their subordinates with a minimum of concession to their physical and emotional needs.

Conditions in the works were unpleasant. The air was hot and ventilation, such as it was, was insufficient. The irksomeness of long hours in the enervating heat and humidity of the workshop was hard to bear, but harder still was the contempt shown to the women by the managers. They insisted that anyone who wished to go to the lavatory during work-time must raise a hand and ask permission. Like children, their bodily functions were to be supervised.

The reason given by the Management was that during a period of refurbishment the normal toilets were not available, and a facility in another building had to be used instead. Workers might take advantage of the inevitably longer time they would have to take over their visits to the toilet to linger out of sight, smoking, chatting and delaying their return to work.

The explanation was insulting in itself, and caused many workers to join the strike (about which a great deal was said and written at the time). My own response to this piece of English industrial mis-management, however, was coloured by my recollection of an altogether grimmer scene described in a book written by a survivor of a German death camp.

He recounted how the Germans made the Jewish prisoners line up outside the communal lavatory to perform their evacuations in public. Since there were many more prisoners than there were places in the lavatory the Germans had appointed a man whom they dressed as a rabbi and labelled 'Scheissmeister' (shitmaster). He was equipped with a large clock with which he timed each person's visit, and he was under the strictest orders to allow no-one to stay longer than his allotted time. If a prisoner took more than a few seconds to ease himself the Scheissmeister had to drive him out of the latrine with a stick. This pantomime caused the Germans endless amusement.

When people have no identity, no dignity and no rights, when they have become beings to whom anything may be done, it seems natural to intrude upon the most intimate and private of their functions. Passing water and defecating, which real people do discreetly, excusing themselves from the company with a polite euphemism, become annoying distractions when children do them. The same is true of any group whom those in power think of as children - employees, prisoners, claimants, refugees, minorities. They are people whose physical and psychological needs have no priority. If they cannot shit and piss at the appointed time - or whatever else it might be convenient to make them do - they must be harassed and demeaned until they can.

The humiliation of underlings

Alice Miller explains that this deep-seated drive to humiliate underlings has its origin in the helpless child every adult person once was. The harm which is caused to social relationships by its vehemence is incalculable. If we could break into the cycle of disordered childhood leading to angry, embittered adulthood, I think it is possible that we could eliminate vast areas of social conflict from our lives in a generation. We could revalue young people and recognise that if treatment such as I have decried would make us angry and resentful it is certain to do the same to children. We could also admit to ourselves that when we are tempted to impose upon other adults behaviours which recall the nursery and the classroom, we are participating in a regressive process which has in recent history led to disaster.

This argument presupposes that abrasive interactions between people are not what nature intended. I suspect that a large proportion of society holds the opposite view, believing that an idealistic hope of realising a society in which conflict and social tension are largely unknown is self-delusive because humanity is simply not made like that. I cannot refute that belief because it is only pseudo-logical, having been created by the very mechanisms which it sustains. It is part of an integral cycle of events which will continue to run as long as nothing breaks into it and successfully refutes its guiding premises. It is a self-fulfilling prophecy.

Such a refutation will only begin to work when the institutions which bring people together and allow them to act on each other, consciously reorganise themselves so as to put respect and free communication far above efficiency in the scale of priorities.

Contempt for workers

Factories and offices exist at present to make wealth for their owners and share-holders. So pressing has the need become to increase profits every year that many enterprises have largely abandoned decent treatment for their workers. Wages have slipped down until they no longer keep poverty at bay. I have met workers who feel as if their employers think of them as irresponsible children, and make a point of 'fining' them or cutting their bonus payments for trivial breaches of factory rules. Inevitably the workers' enthusiasm diminishes and their commitment to high quality work declines. They see no reason to do their best work for employers who hold them in contempt, and do not understand that workers need to feel sustained and strengthened as much by their employers' esteem as by the wages they pay.

Judging the worth of managers by their ability to cut down unit labour costs by squeezing wages and forcing employees to increase their output has embittered labour relations and reduced the efficiency of Britain's economy. No rational friend of this nation, who wanted to see her prosperous and at peace with herself, would favour organising the shop-floor along the abrasive, confrontational lines to which we have become accustomed. Yet the conflict goes on, driven not by reason but by the hidden image of childhood pain, formed when those managers themselves were managed by their parents, and told over and over again that they were untrustworthy, unskilful, needing supervision and correction. No child whose parents loved and respected him, cherishing his individuality and releasing him to try new activities and relationships would want, when he grew up, to treat others any differently.

The industrial chaos which the Thatcher Government thought it had abolished was not caused by subversion or ill-will. It grew in the innumerable abusive families from which came the managers and the workers who fought each other year upon year, re-enacting the psychological struggles of their childhood, and never achieving reconciliation, because parents and children will always be unequal, eternally at odds.

Contempt for offenders

Similar tensions exist in many other areas of life. In prisons and youth custody centres, people who have committed crimes are locked away from their families, which are likely to have been abusive, but while detained they suffer the repressed childhood anger of the prison officers, and so the opportunity to revolutionise their lives by giving them the kindness and respect their inner child craves is lost.

I have often asked myself why imprisonment persists as the foundation-stone of European penology, and why, in spite of increasingly abundant evidence that in many cases it actually encourages offending, responsible politicians still turn to it as a panacea whenever they feel they have to find a serviceable remedy for crime. It is expensive and degrading, which ought to make it unpopular with monetarists and liberals alike, yet even as I write, in the midst of crisis in public finance, more prisons are being built, and more offences are being made imprisonable.

Unfortunately, it also seems to meet a profound affective need in the majority of the population by allowing them to project onto the criminal the sense of outrage and justified indignation created in them as they grew up. As a result we have become used to a pseudo-liberal rhetoric about prison which claims that it accomplishes its whole punitive intention by locking the criminal up so that he suffers restriction and loss of autonomy. This idea is often summed up in the words: 'A criminal goes to prison AS a punishment. He does not go there TO BE punished.'

Whether a prison system based honestly on that principle would be entirely successful in rehabilitating offenders is arguable. Evidence certainly exists that other countries, notably The Netherlands and Sweden, have created prisons which restrain convicts effectively by keeping them under lock and key, but also offer them a tolerant, stimulating environment in which their offending can be challenged. Unfortunately, the English approach to imprisonment is alloyed with a strong sense that its real aim is to corral criminals in an oppressive community where they can be degraded and infantilised. As Robert Sykes, who spent many years in prison, writes:

> *"Sometimes the smell in these triple cells becomes so offensive that the convicts try to smother it by placing their own clothing over the chamber pots at night. The result is that their very clothes become impregnated with the smell. It is quite revolting.*
>
> *At Pentonville the lags got so disgusted that they decided to organise a mass filth campaign in an attempt to bring about some improvements in the vile conditions. In a mass demonstration of protest they began hurling the contents of the chamber pots out of*

the cell windows until the exercise yards and grounds looked like laystalls.

Some lags went even further and tipped the contents of their chamber pots over the heads of the screws. This is all quite revolting, but if the prison authorities take the last vestige of human decency away from men how do they expect them to behave? How a supposedly enlightened Home Office and conscientious Prison Commissioners can tolerate such an abominable state of affairs without taking drastic steps to remedy it is beyond my comprehension."

(Robert Sykes, (1967) *Who's Been Eating My Porridge?* p.96)

Another writer, Anthony Heckstall-Smith, confirms the soul-destroying effect of deliberately imposed degradation:

"Presently my own cell was unlocked. I took a tentative glance outside. Men carrying chamber-pots, basins and buckets, trooped past. Emptying my slops into the stinking chamber, I followed them and joined the long queue that was forming at the recess in which were a lavatory and a large sink, with a cold water tap, into which the men emptied their chambers. The stench was nauseating and soon the stone floor was swimming with spilt urine and water.

"The f---er's stopped up again" one of the prisoners told me. "Some c---t's thrown 'is cob darn it!"

By the time I reached it, the sink was filled to the brim and overflowing. On the top of it floated a layer of human excreta. Retching, I turned away and threw the contents of my pot down the lavatory."

(Anthony Heckstall-Smith, (1954) *Eighteen Months*)

If the prison officers who administer the prisons in which these conditions existed, and for all I know still exist, had been able to express at the right time their own feelings about the experience of powerless subjection which they endured as children they would not allow anyone to tell them that a fellow human being deserved to be locked up with his chamber-pot and left to defecate in public like a baby going through potty training. They would find such an identity of emotion with the prisoners that they would make the prison ungovernable until proper sanitation was installed.

Only people who have split off and locked away in the fastnesses of their mind the honest anger aroused in them by their parents' heavy-handed manipulation of their immature bodies and minds could break the natural links of empathy and concern for others. These are the links which cause normal people to be distressed when they see men and women suffering degradation which they themselves would rather die than endure.

The tragedy of our time is, I believe, that those of our institutions which concern themselves with the kind of lives people lead - schools, hospitals, prisons, dole offices - are usually run by individuals whose behaviour is governed at its source by anger transformed but not attenuated during its growth, into 'reasonable, common-sense, robust attitudes' towards those who find themselves cast against their will in the perilous role of Children.

Chapter four

Unrecognised abuse

Child abuse has forced itself into our consciousness in recent years. It has become a normal item of news. Through admirable initiatives such as Esther Rantzen's Childline young people have started the hard work of revealing how adults have imposed on them painful and humiliating ill-treatment. We have been confronted by evidence that adults who put young people through physical and emotional torture are not rare, isolated monsters but outwardly normal people, often professionals or parents.

This horrifying truth baffles us. We are culturally predisposed to expect evil to declare itself, to wear horns and smell of sulphur. If it is decked out in the garments of bourgeois normality, if it hides its identity under a cloak of social worthiness, as it does when teachers, scoutmasters, heads of children's homes and the like do it, we first deny its reality and then, when it is no longer possible to disbelieve, we punish the guilty savagely enough to convince ourselves that they are, in fact, still in a class apart, and nothing remotely like the rest of us.

Yet, as Dr. Miller has striven to show us, abuse is more than sexual interference. By isolating the sexual component of child abuse and making it the archetypal crime against the young, those who mould public opinion have prevented us from perceiving how often children suffer from abuse which is not even remotely sexual. Alice Miller is at pains to declare that much which passes for traditional, devoted child-rearing is no less abusive than the vile activities of paedophiles. The mechanism which compels small children to submit body and soul to their parents and in later years to forget they have done so ensures that even when one controversial form of child-abuse becomes known and forbidden, the others remain hidden, sanctified by custom and endlessly forced upon children 'for their own good'.

What is this non-sexual child-abuse? I confess that I approach the answer to that question with fear and trembling, because I have to say that when all the excuses and special pleading have been given their proper weight it seems to me that most of what adults do to their children between the ages of nought and sixteen is either essentially abusive, or capable of becoming so if they do it thoughtlessly, in response to their own unrecognised emotions.

At the beginning of her book *For your own good* (Virago), Alice Miller quotes extensively from books written in the eighteenth and nineteenth century by German 'experts' on child-rearing. Read against a background of modern liberal thinking they are almost comic. They express vividly the conviction, embodied in such Victorian books as 'Tom Brown's Schooldays' and 'Eric, or Little By Little', that children are born savage, racked by evil impulses, devious and manipulative. Only harsh treatment, underpinned by the moral and spiritual austerities of evangelical Christianity, can remould the child's degenerate soul.

The religious sanctioning of child abuse

In our post-religious age, (I mean, an age in which religion no longer furnishes the dominant images by which society defines its fundamental purposes) we would probably see the following passage as quaint:

> *'True love flows from the heart of God, the source and image of all fatherhood (Ephesians 3:15), is revealed and prefigured in the love of the Redeemer, and is engendered, nourished and preserved in man by the Spirit of Christ. This love emanating from above purifies, sanctifies, transfigures and strengthens natural parental love. This hallowed love has as its primary goal the growth of the child's interior self, his spiritual life, his liberation from the power of the flesh, his elevation above the demands of the merely natural life of the senses, his inner independence from the world threatening to engulf him. Therefore this love is concerned that the child learn at an early age to renounce, control and master himself, that he not blindly follow the promptings of the flesh and the senses but rather the higher will and the promptings of the spirit. This hallowed love can be severe even as it can be mild, can deny even as it can bestow,*

> *each according to its time; it also knows* **how to bring good by**
> **causing hurt** *(emphasis mine), it can impose harsh renunciation*
> *like a physician who prescribes bitter medicine, like a surgeon*
> *who knows very well that the cut of his knife will cause pain and*
> *yet cuts in order to save a life. "Thou shalt beat him (the child)*
> *with a rod, and shalt deliver his soul from hell" (Proverbs 23:14)*
> *With these words, Solomon reveals to us that* **true love can also**
> **be severe** *(emphasis mine).*[1]
> (K.A. Schmid, ed. Enzyklopadie des gesamten Erziehungs- und
> Unterrichtswesens [A Comprehensive Encyclopedia of Education
> and Instruction], 1887)[1]

Yet shorn of its religious cloaking the attitude towards children which is set out
in Schmid's writing - that they must be held down, compelled to submit and
firmly discouraged from expressing unauthorised or inconvenient feelings - is
very little different from the assumptions which rule the lives of many children
today, both at home and at school. The message which Schmid conveyed to
parents of Alois Hitler's generation is still being passed on and faithfully
operated against youngsters today. It is this: if you are a parent you cannot
possibly be mistaken if you forbid, deny, suppress or punish. The effectiveness
of your parenting can be gauged precisely by the amount of resistance it
encounters from the child, and by the distress it causes him.

We are, of course, more enlightened today than people were when Schmid was
writing. We temper the monastic ferocity of our discipline in response to the
promptings of the moderately liberal civilisation in which we live, and our
relative prosperity tends to break the link which certainly existed in former
times between the inescapable stringency of life in a poverty-stricken
community and the idea that children need to learn self-denial. Nonetheless,
we see in the daily life of late twentieth-century Europe much that ought to be
recognised as stemming from the same roots as what has gone before.

Freedom and control

I have noticed that whenever I suggest to parents that children need freedom in
which to discover how they are uniquely equipped to live, I receive an answer
which is almost always the same, and often expressed in the same words: "Do
you mean that I should let my child go and play on a busy road (or sometimes "

on the Motorway") if he/she wants to?" I should emphasise that this question is not asked in the context of a discussion about road safety: it always emerges from talk about libertarian parenting. It suggests to me either that most parents sincerely believe all the thwarting, controlling and punishing they do is absolutely necessary to save their children from hazards which might threaten their lives, or that they are using the road-safety argument, because of its air of responsible rationality, to conceal their recognition that their relations with their children are governed by dark, essentially cruel motives.

I honestly do not know which is the true motivation. Perhaps both operate at times. The unanimity of the response, however, suggests to me very strongly that parents have common experiences from which they form their ideas of children's nature. People who had been trusted and valued when they were children, people whose parents had made an effort to give them freedom within secure natural boundaries would not conceive children in negative terms.

They would not see the natural curiosity of children as a self-destructive drive, destined to destroy both the youngster's physical existence and the power-relationship to which his parents attach so much importance. They would be able to recognise the simple fact that the emotions of children are no less pressing and humanly authentic than those of adults. From this recognition they would be able to deduce that their children, far from actively campaigning to overthrow their parents, love them dearly, with the love of the totally helpless for the one who can ensure their safety, and wish only to have their feelings recognised and cherished.

No justice for children

How different that response is from what has been understood as the 'right' way to handle children's emotions! In many years of observing and working with children I can say that I have almost never seen an adult who could tolerate a child being angry because of the way that adult had treated him. Children are allowed to be distressed, for a short time at least, over the pain of an accidental injury. They may be briefly upset when hurt by another child. But let them dare to strike back, even verbally, if their parents hit them, or punish them in some other way, and a tempest of 'righteous' anger will very likely burst over them.

From this they soon learn that for children there is no justice, no equal treatment before the Law, no recognition that if it is hard for an adult to accept the thwarting of his deepest needs *a fortiori* it is almost impossible for a young child. Yet without the right to express fully their feelings, children never overcome repression.

Because our Society has accepted almost without criticism the assumption that children do not feel for more than a few seconds at any one time, we have failed, as a community, to develop an understanding of how our behaviour towards our children affects them. We do not recognise their vulnerability and therefore we cannot apply that recognition to the structures in which we bring them up.

An example of this indifference to children's feelings is the conviction many parents express that 'Children do not know what is good for them.' This is a restatement of the concept behind the question, 'Would you let your child play on the Motorway?' It presupposes that because children do not necessarily recognise all the natural and artificial dangers with which adults have filled the world, they cannot ever be trusted to decide on a course of action to which their adult carers do not consent, and pursue it. The reasoning I hear very often from adults whom I challenge on this point goes as follows:

> *- You wouldn't let him play on the Motorway, would you?*

> *- No. That is not a question of freedom. Freedom is not the same as destructive lunacy.*

> *- Well, if you accept that he cannot be allowed to choose that course of action because he does not have enough experience to know what is safe for him you must also allow us to take all the other decisions which affect him, because he is ignorant in those areas too.*

Thinking like this sounds responsible and humane. In the mouth of a judge, a social worker or a teacher it passes for unchallengeable good sense. Yet examined more closely it reveals the same cancerous denial of reality which has worked against human happiness since the earliest times.

To say of a child that he 'does not know what is good for him' is the same as saying 'his emotions do not exist; his perception of the world around him is not merely imperfect, it is an illusion. Not only does he not know that electricity may shock him to death or fast cars run him over but he even thinks that he is not tired when adults say he is, and send him to bed, and he falsely assumes that the pain he feels when he is 'spanked', and the indignation that arouses in him entitle him to arraign the people who have hurt him before the bar of justice.' Such an idea is nonsensical.

Expressed even more trenchantly, this assertion of the child's incapacity means 'Children are exactly what adults say they are. If I, an adult, think a child is 'naughty', then that is what he is. His naughtiness is as real as a burglary or a murder. It is proved against him, by evidence as strong as a signed confession. No mitigation is possible if I refuse to consider it, and no-one would criticise me if I did not, since it is important to see that children 'do not learn to talk their way out of trouble.'

The reader may assert that this is not how he sees his role as an adult or a parent. He may say that all his relationships with children are governed by his love for them, and that the times when he has to control or punish a young person are regrettable but necessary because that young person has simply failed in his duty. He must learn that when he grows up he will not be able to do as he wishes all the time; there will be employers and policemen, tax-inspectors and dole-clerks who will expect him to co-operate with them, and he must not grow up thinking he is his own person, not linked into the network of institutional constraints without which a modern society cannot work.

Charter for slavery

Sensible though this sounds, it is a charter for slavery. Because every adult begins life as a defenceless child, the smallest, weakest, most ignorant and incapable member of the family in which he grows up, his earliest, and inevitably strongest impressions of what it is to be human are framed by that sense of helplessness. It is that sense which he projects upon children. Just as no-one listened to him and took his frustration and his bewilderment seriously when he was young so he relegates his children to the status of powerless unpersons.

It is normal for the powerless to seek power. Equally normal is the desire of those who rule over them to keep power out of their hands. The conflict between them is self-renewing, as we have seen. But to make a virtue of it, to carry it on in the name of God, or Morality, or Civic Responsibility is surely hypocritical.

But such hypocrisy is rooted in our society. It perpetuates fruitless, sometimes murderous conflicts between the generations, and worst of all it blights the mental health of those who will bear responsibility for defending the freedoms which we and our predecessors have won. Their maturity and their benevolence are the only bulwarks we have against fascism. As Alice Miller says in *Banished Knowledge* (page 176):

> *'On the basis of the pedagogy that was practised on us, the exerting of unlimited power by the adult over the child is still taken for granted. Most people know nothing else. It is only from a child who was never injured that we can learn entirely new, honest and truly humane behaviour. Such a child does not accept without question the pedagogic reasoning to which we are susceptible. He feels he is entitled to ask questions, to demand explanations, to stand up for himself and to articulate his needs.'*

School and the perpetuation of resentment

At this point I am tempted to let the argument rest, with Alice Miller's summary of the challenge we face as a civilised society. My own commitment to education, however, impels me to go on a step.

If we accept Dr. Miller's contention that children grow up into kindly, self-confident adults only if they are respected and allowed to articulate their feelings during childhood, we must ask ourselves whether the arrangements we make for their education have any chance of achieving that end. If they do not they must be recognised as time-wasting at best and dangerous at worst.

Most children go to school. What arrangements are made in the average school for children who find that the way they are treated wakens in them strong and painful emotions? Is there a forum in which they can express their needs openly and candidly? Is it possible for young people to tell their teachers when their lessons are boring or difficult to follow, or when the mechanisms by which they control their classes are hurtful? Is it safe in our schools for the pupils to say openly and in an atmosphere of common respect that, either because of misunderstanding or thoughtlessness, the responsible adults in their lives have hurt them? And does the school recognise that truth, even when it is told by children, is valuable and should never be a source of danger?

If the answer to any of these questions is 'no', I have to say seriously, and with a sober consciousness, that I am treading on holy ground, that schooling is undoubtedly a cause of the social anguish it is supposed to alleviate. Even if it produces scholars and scientists, it does no good to the human society it serves if those highly educated people cannot love, and harbour dammed-up, repressed resentments whose only possible mode of expression is the harsh rearing and punitive control of everyone whose position places them into the generic role of children.

It amazes me that so many serious educators accept the level of tension their pupils seem to endure every day. When I was teaching I remember vividly how drawn and strained the children were, and how often they reacted to me as if I were their sworn enemy because I was the source of that tension, and the cause of their suffering. I was not always an inspired teacher, especially when, towards the end of my career, I began to doubt the value or utility of teaching, but I do not think the children's malaise was caused entirely by my shortcomings. In fact, as I recounted in *Compulsory Schooling Disease* I sometimes became the conduit for deep-seated indignation about the way teachers treated pupils, simply because I had given the impression that I was a safe person to tell these things to. The schools I taught in were, without exception filled with unhappy, tense and angry children. Shamefully, the teachers who worked in them almost never acknowledged the hurtful effect of their repressive, restrictive regime on the young minds and unformed personalities whose education had been entrusted to them.

Provoking antagonism

Worst of all, young people are denied justice. When the tension consequent on school life becomes unbearable, some children resist it by refusing to do what the teacher tells them. Instead of recognising, as they would if they were really conscious of their pupils' humanity, that they, the teachers, have provoked the antagonism which their pupils show, they react as if the youngsters who disrupt their classes have chosen to do so out of simple wickedness. They blame the children for behaviour which they would themselves display if someone took over their lives for five or six hours a day and made them listen to endless talk about things which did not interest them.

It is remarkable that when adults run courses or conferences they take care to see that the participants, all of mature age, are not subjected to a programme of activities even remotely as intensive or heavy as a normal school day. They are offered coffee and a chance to relax at regular intervals. They are spoken to respectfully, and their opinion is listened to with attention. Adults, who have at least the experience and maturity to put up with hardship in the course of getting useful knowledge, never seem to need those things. Children, who by nature have fewer psychological resources and far less experience of life, bear without support or help a gruelling daily obstacle-course compounded of long, demanding lessons, frequent arbitrary changes of subject, disturbing tests and constant pressure from adults to stop doing the things which come naturally to their minds.

I ask the educational world why it still believes that this scheme of things has value, and that it is entitled to stigmatise children who resist it. I find it harder and harder to understand why a community which no longer tolerates doctors who bleed and purge their patients instead of finding out what is wrong with them and treating it properly smiles on teachers who hound non-conforming pupils without trying seriously to discern why they are unhappy and obstructive.

By the same token it amazes me that schools, which are undoubtedly run by intelligent, even sensitive, people, do not see that accumulated hurts and grievances, such as many pupils show clearly that they have, cannot fail to create in them anger and a deep yearning for justice. I find growing in me a feeling of outrage that so many decent young people leave our schools, after eleven years of compulsory instruction, with their deepest needs, those which exert the strongest effect on their psychological and emotional growth, unmet.

Honesty and clear-sightedness must quickly replace triumphalist adult authoritarianism as the dominant motif of English education. If they do not, we may well see a generation growing up which has little or no love, and scant reserves of kindness with which to nurture their own children.

Societal influences which traditionally restrained and channelled rooted anger and frustration - religion, conscription, settled patriarchal family life sustained by abundant, though often low-paid employment, have weakened or disappeared. Technology, both elaborate and relatively inexpensive, has filled homes with exciting and desirable entertainment machines, and from them has grown up a culture made up largely of ephemeral but expensive items like games and pop-music discs. Getting these things, or acquiring the money to buy them, legally or otherwise, has become a consuming passion for many young people, and the gratification which they offer takes the place of normal human love in many of their lives. It is not hard to visualise a world in which young people who have only ever learned to assuage the daily irritation of life as powerless underlings by scraping their nerve-endings with synthetic excitements grow into a nation of hardened thrill-seekers utterly impervious to love, to warmth and to human need.

Chapter five

Knowledge, honesty and a healthy society

A recurrent theme in Alice Miller's work is the obsessive concealment of truth which leads to disastrous violence and lifelong anguish. She tells, from her own experience, of how difficult it is to drive a wedge of fearless veracity into the common tradition which governs child-rearing in our society, to insist that to inflict pain or humiliation upon another person without his informed consent cannot ever be justified and to allow children to reveal freely that it has happened to them.

My own observation confirms Dr. Miller's impression that our lives are tightly governed by the provisions of a law so fundamental and universal it never needs to be stated because everyone obeys it without thinking. It holds that wherever there is a relation analogous to Parent and Child in any social situation, the Parent figure must be protected from protest, criticism or resistance from the Child. The Parent's behaviour must always be interpreted pedagogically, that is to say, as a benevolent action intended to produce a future benefit for the Child by modifying his behaviour so as to make it more 'moral' or obedient to the dominant social code.

Although it encompasses the family and the school, this Law's field of application is by no means restricted to those areas. It affects gross interactions within the Community, including the following:

PARENT	CHILD
Government	The electorate
Employers	Employees
Professionals	Clients
(Pro tem) Conservatives	Other Parties
Britons	Foreigners/Immigrants

and it produces corrosive responses of a precisely similar kind in each case.

In fact, as I observed in a previous chapter, the tension produced by the mechanisms of blocked need and the refusal of warmth in childhood may actually tend to generate similar speech-patterns when adults revive the pain they were unable to feel and express when they were young. Certainly I notice that Parent-figures seem to adopt a diction very like the way a parent speaks to his child when they address themselves to those they see as subordinate. One only has to listen for a short while to a British Prime Minister speaking to the nation on television - Margaret Thatcher is a vivid example, but almost any other would do as well - to hear the forceful, manipulative tones of a parent handling a child.

If the behaviour of the Parent is 'programmed' by his role in the drama of the Unhappy Child, that of the Child himself is no less predictable. Enmeshed in the struggle to bring out into open view the despair and indignation engendered by their early experience of being suppressed, both at home and at school, people in the Child position often resist, even when to do so may lead directly to their being harmed or impoverished, so strong is the impulse to find ways of speaking honestly to their parental oppressors.

How else can we explain the role played by strikes in the history of Trade Relations, an archetypal arena of relived childhood drama? A strike is a infirm weapon at the best of times: it hurts and undermines those who use it at least as much as those at whom it is aimed. In fact, nowadays employers even find it worthwhile to provoke strikes - the last great Miners' Strike is an example - in order to have an excuse for closing works and dismissing staff when they feel the need to do so. Yet the strike continues to be the weapon of choice at least for the more old-fashioned Trade Union leaders. Perhaps this is because it gives expression to the longing of every repressed child to say, "No, I won't do what you tell me! I refuse to bow to you any more. Even if I suffer because of my rebellion, I shall at least have found a way to keep my dignity and my right to act as I see fit."

I cannot 'prove' that what I say is 'true' in the sense that scientific laws are 'true'. Others, like the elaborators of Transactional Analysis, have observed similar behaviours in people and erected their insights into a system of therapy. I am in no position to do that. I can only offer my intuitions and pursue them to the point of asking WHY people feel as they do, and WHY the same constructs recur in a variety of cases. As I said at the beginning of this chapter, I think the answer can be found in the prevalence of dishonesty and covertness in our civilisation.

Real knowledge is the enemy of pedagogy

I watched a popular television show in which a presenter invited a number of people with strong opinions to discuss the age at which sex education should be offered to children. The argument followed a well-trodden path. Several young people spoke of their early sexual experience. Some had been taught about contraception, and had avoided having unwanted children: others had not, and wanted to say that they regretted very much having been left to discover by bitter experience that unprotected sex can precipitate at least one partner into a lifetime of responsibility for which she may not be ready. As far as I could see, the case for better sex education was proved.

Opposed to these young people were some older women. One was a right-wing Conservative, well-known for her championship of opposition to nuclear disarmament. Another looked like Victoria Gillick, who campaigned against doctors advising girls under sixteen about sex without telling their parents. As I listened to their impassioned harangue, I was struck not only by the way they ignored the good, practical points made by their opponents, but also how angry and bewildered they seemed to be at the idea that anyone could disagree with them.

Their argument was, in essence, that children and young people are 'innocent' as long as no-one tells them anything about sex until they reach an unspecified, but late, age. What these women meant by 'innocent' was not articulated clearly: few youngsters pass through childhood without experiencing some sexual feelings; fewer still avoid hearing fragments of information about sex transmitted to them through playground folklore. So the 'innocent' child cannot be said to be insulated from sex. This 'innocence' consists of not having been formally admitted to the circle of those who know things only adults should know. I suspect that, without realising it, these women were not discussing sex at all, but power and its relationship to knowledge.

I think they were disturbed and angry not because it had been suggested that children should learn about sex, but because they might learn it from the wrong people, teachers or doctors, who might thus detach the youngsters from their subjection to their parents and initiate them prematurely into adulthood.

Experts in counselling explained clearly that young people who had been given straightforward information about sex tended to have fewer unwanted children. Indeed, it emerged that, in spite of - or perhaps because of - our cultural resistance to sex education, Britain had a higher rate of teenage pregnancy than any other European country.

None of these arguments diminished the evangelical ardour of the older women. Stirred up by moral panic, they shouted and harangued, growing more and more angry as their opponents remained unshaken. It was a predictable and unedifying encounter. To me, however, its message was unambiguous: there is a rooted opposition in our culture to the idea of children being freed to negotiate their own intellectual commerce with the world around them.

This resistance comes about, I believe, because real knowledge, obtained independently by self-managed experience, is the implacable enemy of pedagogy. Pedagogy - the subjection of the mind and the moulding of the personality by another person in harmony with that person's intentions - is the foundation stone of all our political, social and educational life. To dethrone it is to risk the destruction of a world-view which, although it is based on the painful, oppressive experiences so many ordinary people had to endure when they were young, is at least familiar, common and thoroughly elaborated.

People who, like the anti-sex education lobby, see themselves as bulwarks of the existing order, cannot easily put aside comforting thought-patterns formed at the most impressionable stage of their lives.

Reform society to respect the truth

Yet if we do not meet the challenge to make forbidden knowledge available, if we do not courageously reform society so that children learn at the very beginning of their existence to tell their truth and demand that those around them do the same, we risk seeing the present system continue.

In that system children suffer interminable pain, they are humiliated, stultified and subjected so that their natural confidence and intellectual power are more or less destroyed by the time they reach adulthood. They become inured to failure and inadequacy, and worst of all they often come to assume that no-one will ever speak the truth to them or believe what they say. Consequently they begin to adopt the cynical outlook which in due course they will use in their relations with their own children.

If as a nation we could overcome the deposit of concentrated distress laid down in the lives of many adults when they experienced their parents' deafness to their real needs, we might learn to revalue our children. At present the dominant influence over their lives, both at home and at school, is their parents' grandiose desire to assert control over them, ostensibly for their own good but in reality because the adults have internalised the contemptuous rejection they experienced from THEIR parents and transformed it into a high-handed tutelage.

The image of child-nature which flows from that tutelage justifies all the dishonesty, the manipulation and the concealment which goes on between parents and children. It encourages adults to think of children as incapable, insensitive and irresponsible beings, who cannot be taken seriously.

Their relative inarticulacy, taken together with their small size and their high voices allows adults to assume that what children say need not be taken seriously, unless it happens to agree with what the adults think they ought to say. Children are often impulsive. Because adults like to think that, as grown-ups, they plan their own lives and evaluate their actions carefully, (a questionable assertion in some cases) it is easy for them to misinterpret the habit many young people have of rushing from activity to activity, showing enormous enthusiasm for a short time but not finishing anything. It seems to them that the youngsters ought to have the same attitude as they do, and if they do not, it is part of a parent's responsibility to make them change.

One of the most grievous mistreatments adults mete out to children is their habit of assuming that they do not really mean what they say. Countless times in my life as a teacher I have been told: "Don't take what the kids say seriously. They don't really mean it. They are just trying to manipulate you." Or a mother may say to me about her small child: "He's only crying to draw attention to himself. He's perfectly happy really. He just wants to make me stop what I'm doing and see to him." If I challenge this statement I am often told: "I know my own child better than you. I live with him twenty-four hours a day. If I say he's attention-seeking you can be sure he is!"

What a universe of contempt is compressed into words like those. To say to any human being that his feelings, and the words with which he gives them expression have no standing, no sincerity, is surely a fundamental breach of his essential rights. It places him in the position of a person struggling to breathe in an enclosed space, howling in despair, while outside people who could open his prison and release him from his agony stare at him in amused curiosity but turn aside, affecting to think that he is, in fact, only play-acting.

Listening to the feelings

It is only since I left the teaching profession that I have been able to see how easy it is to take another, very different, line of approach to children. I have learned to listen, not to the words children say, but to the feelings which those words convey. I have also learned to wait for youngsters to finish what they are saying, even if they have to make several attempts to express themselves fully. Most important of all, I have learned to take very seriously how they feel at the moment of speaking, and to make them aware that I will not high-handedly impose my own wishes on them because I am an adult and think I know better than they do what is good for them.

I find that when I treat them like this, children quickly begin to behave with a new poise and confidence in their ability to learn. I have seen them develop more complex, adult ways of speaking when the opportunity to use them arises. I have watched children raised in freedom by parents who respect and approve of them go for hours without either wasting time or being bored. I have watched them build their lives without the conflicts which our culture insists are inevitable during adolescence. I know from experience that if you tell the truth to your children and show them that you recognise in them not only the small, undeveloped person they are at the moment, but also the strong, confident adult they have the power to become, and even the old, wise, experienced person they may be towards the end of their life, they respond like concentration-camp inmates liberated after a long imprisonment.

As a foster-carer I have tested this approach out in practice. Although I have found that no-one, however radical and thoroughgoing, can completely undo the corrosion caused by mishandling during the most impressionable years of a person's life, it is possible to treat even damaged children in a way which strengthens their sociable impulses and encourages them to move away from the common patterns of adolescent behaviour.

I have rarely been abused openly by the youngsters I have fostered. They have stolen from me, lied to me when the situation led them to, and even made false accusations against me. But in their normal social relationships with me they have almost always avoided the kind of open abuse which boils up in many families to the point where the parents throw the children out.

I try always to speak to them as if I think of them as my equals. If I have to impose on them I always try my best to explain that, whatever my own feelings may be I am bound by regulations which force me to act in certain ways, even though my own wishes might be different. I always try to ensure that whatever rules I feel there should be in my house apply to me as much as to them. I always tell them where I am going, and try to let them know if I change my plans, because that is what I expect of them. They do not always do it, but I have been impressed by the number of times even a really difficult boy has phoned me to let me know he will be late. Above all, I avoid moralising. I try to show the boys that if they steal from me it hurts me, and they have to decide whether they care enough for me not to want me hurt. If they do not, I have some more work to do. If they do I want them to know exactly how their conduct affects me, so that they can change it.

I do not suggest that I have found a perfect way to repair the damage society does to its children, and eventually to the adults they become. I have not, partly because I have not quite cast off all the prejudices I got from my own childhood. Although I suspect that the pilfering some children do whenever the opportunity arises represents their symbolic attempt to wrest love from their parents, of whom I am a convenient representative, I still feel shocked and angry when it happens to me. Tolerating damaged children is still not the easiest thing in the world for me. At the very least, however, I recognise that it must be done.

Although I had been thinking along these lines for a while before I began to read Alice Miller's books, it was in them that I found the clearest, most heart-warming exposition of the viewpoint towards which I was groping. At the end of some of her books I found an appendix containing a sort of Creed for people who are serious about transforming Society by revising their attitudes towards children. The whole text is worth reading, but the sections which bear most strongly upon the argument of this chapter are these:

1. All children are born to grow, to develop, to live, to love, and to articulate their needs and feelings for their self-protection.

2. For their development, children need the respect and protection of adults who take them seriously, love them and honestly help them to become orientated in the world.

3. When these vital needs are frustrated and children are instead abused for the sake of adults' needs by being exploited, beaten, punished, taken advantage of, manipulated, neglected or deceived without the intervention of any witness, then their integrity will be lastingly impaired.

4. The normal reactions to such injury should be anger and pain; since children are forbidden to express their anger and since it would be unbearable to experience their pain all alone, they are compelled to suppress their feelings, repress all memory of the trauma, and idealise those guilty of abuse. Later they will have *no memory of what was done to them* (emphasis Alice Miller's).

5. Dissociated from the original cause, their feelings of anger, helplessness, despair, longing, anxiety and pain will find expression in destructive acts against others (criminal behaviour, mass murder) or against themselves (drug addiction, alcoholism, prostitution, psychic disorders, suicide).

6. If these people become parents, they will often direct acts of revenge for their mistreatment in childhood against their own children, whom they use as scapegoats. Child abuse is still sanctioned - indeed, held in high regard - in our Society, as long as it is defined as child-rearing. It is a tragic fact that parents beat their children in order to escape the emotions stemming from how they were treated by their own parents.

and particularly,

7. If mistreated children are not to become criminals or mentally ill, it is essential that *at least once in their life* (emphasis Alice Miller's) they come into contact with a person who knows *without any doubt* (emphasis mine) that the environment, not the helpless, battered child, is at fault. In this regard, knowledge or ignorance on the part of Society can be instrumental in either saving or destroying as life. Here lies the great opportunity for relatives, social workers, therapists, teachers, doctors, psychiatrists, officials and nurses to support the child and *to believe her or him* (emphasis Alice.Miller's).

Chapter six

Changing things

One of my younger friends, a home-schooled child, was using me to learn French. When I was a teacher I used to think that I had to 'cover' a certain number of new concepts, and revise so many old ones in each lesson, so I was taken aback, for a second at least, when after a rather short session the lad asked me to stop because he had done enough for now. He felt his interest in French had been assuaged for the moment and he wanted to go and play.

He spoke politely. I told him that he was in charge, and that I wanted to know at every stage, exactly what he wanted to learn, and when he needed to finish learning. I was not put out or worried because I knew that he was serious, willing and interested. But he had made me think.

I realised that the boy's request was a) absolutely necessary if he was to learn properly, and b) only possible for me to accept because he was not in school and I was not a paid servant of a Local Education Authority. If he had been a school pupil I should have had to treat his wish to stop learning as a rebellion against my authority. I should have been expected to tell him that as long as he was a pupil in my class he would do as he was told, learn what I gave him to learn, and not question my superiority. I should have had a duty to turn him into a wrongdoer, which he certainly was not by any moral code that I recognise.

Had he been a schoolboy he would probably have learned a number of ploys intended either to make me think he was complying with my orders, or to create some kind of exciting diversion. The very fact that he knew his mind well enough to recognise when it had received sufficient information made him dangerous to mainstream education. Yet he is not even remotely dangerous. On the contrary, he is a pleasant, self-possessed person. It is the institutional culture of the school which would have made him a deviant, if he had had the misfortune to be caught up in it.

This incident, and many others like it, brought me to a realisation that I have a responsibility. I ask the reader to forgive me if I seem arrogant, but I have to say that I should be surprised if there were more than a small number of professional educators who could have reacted as I did. I say this not because I think a great deal of myself and my attitudes, but simply because I know from experience that our culture does not allow a teacher to defer to a child.

Consequently, teachers develop a rationale in which allowing children to govern the course of their own education has to be seen as absurd. I have learnt during my own professional development, that far from the traditional practice being sensible and correct, it is the tiny minority of educators who recognise the vital necessity of respecting the child's autonomy who have grasped the true nature of their responsibility. Anyone who is certain, as I am, that he has discovered a means of making human life happier, is surely obliged to share what he has learned, as the Talmud says, 'for the sake of peace'.

Every persecutor was once a victim

It seems certain to me that the habit of forcing people to do things against their will comes not from good, logical thought, but from a general experience seeded throughout society in every generation by the unrecognised, unlived, utterly repressed torment of the adults who control everything.

Alice Miller expresses the cause and the cure for this aching poison thus:

> *"If an adult has been fortunate enough to get back to the sources of specific injustice he suffered in his childhood and experience it on a conscious level, then in time he will realise on his own - preferably without the aid of any pedagogical or religious exhortations - that in most cases his parents did not torment or abuse him out of sheer strength and vitality, but because they could not help it, since they were once victims themselves, and thus believed in traditional methods of childrearing.*
>
> *It is very difficult for people to believe the simple fact that EVERY PERSECUTOR WAS ONCE A VICTIM. Yet it should be obvious that someone who was allowed to feel free and strong*

from childhood does not have the need to humiliate another
person."
(Alice Miller (1987) *For Your Own Good*, Virago)

Using these insights to bring about change is never going to be easy. The people who need to remould their beliefs are deeply involved in conservative professions which bar from promotion precisely those people who are most sensitive to the real needs of those they have to work on. For years, even centuries, our social organisations have been developed by means of a consensus dominated by folk who are impelled by the hidden rage of childhood. This drives them to regard determination and intolerance of others' weaknesses as the best qualities, and concession, kindness and flexibility as dangerous weaknesses.

Self-understanding will not come to those who decide the direction of our society as long as the few who have fought their way to a vision of the reality which generated their tormented feelings look on their discovery as a freakish, private insight, good for them but of no interest to anyone else. We need, as a community, to hear in a more concerted way from the reservoirs of confident liberalism which have always existed, but which have in recent years been thrust into the margin by triumphalist authoritarianism.

An end to physical punishment of children

A hopeful development is the formation of EPOCH (End Physical Punishment Of Children). This group emerged after the dissolution of STOPP (Society of Teachers Opposed to Physical Punishment), which followed the abolition of corporal punishment in English State schools. As well as its general aim of persuading parents to use non-violent methods in rearing their children it campaigns for all forms of physical punishment to be made illegal.

This has already happened in a small number of other countries, mainly Scandinavian. It has not led to chaos or an increase in juvenile delinquency. On the contrary, a new culture of child-rearing is taking root there in which parents are beginning to regard hitting children as a rather shameful aberration. Although the Law has been changed to make illegal treatment of children which had previously been accepted by most people as proper and healthy, parents have not been prosecuted in great numbers. That has not been necessary, perhaps because the abolitionist countries have large stable populations of law-abiding people who needed no more than a prompting from the legislature to find good alternatives to beating.

As a result of the dwindling away of direct violence towards children in these countries, it is reported that parents are discovering better, more humane ways to affect their children's behaviour. Instead of blows, these parents are learning to use words to negotiate with their youngsters, who in their turn lose their fear of expressing their point of view. Social work agencies report fewer assaults on children and a general improvement in the tenor of family relationships.

Such a lightening of the atmosphere in which children are brought up could not fail to improve relationships in other areas of life. As Alice Miller has shown:

> *"The child's intense anger at the parents, being strictly forbidden, is simply deflected onto other people and onto himself, but not done away with. Instead, because it is permissible to discharge this anger onto one's children, it spreads over the entire world like a plague."*
> (Alice Miller (1987) *For Your Own Good* Virago p. 248)

The opposite must also be true. When children grow up without the un-endurable but inescapable pain caused by being beaten, they experience less of the anger such pain cannot fail to produce. They mature into adults without having had to mobilise themselves to deal with psychological storm-conditions so achingly familiar to the unfortunate children who every day risk whatever form of arbitrary physical torment their parents choose to inflict on them in support of their private concept of justice.

Consequently, they feel significantly more benevolent towards other members of the community because their parents have enabled them to project onto those people positive, respectful attributes. Freed from the intermittently fearful captivity in which many children live out their lives, they lack the will to oppress which underlies many relationships in the rest of society.

As long as adults refuse to sympathise with their children, we shall not, I think, see the radical changes in our child-rearing culture which will be needed if we are to be protected in the next century from yet another seamless round of abuse, repression and renewed violence. By 'sympathise' I mean 'consciously use their own childhood feelings to share their children's point of view'.

The adults I observe with their youngsters seem very largely to have forgotten how atrociously they were themselves hurt by words and actions which seemed trivial to THEIR elders. It is as if, in growing up, they crossed from one community, the underclass of children, leaving behind all the bonds of solidarity and mutual support which they found there, to another, the adult aristocracy, where they adopted eagerly the oppressive attitudes which had embittered their lives when they had to suffer them. Clearly childhood was no 'golden land' for them, if their grim commitment to harassing their own children is any clue to the origin of their behaviour.

This pervasive culture which allows adults to dehumanise children will not change until it is challenged openly. It is not enough for liberal-minded people to campaign against cruelties such as corporal punishment and compulsory schooling, as if it were possible to achieve a civilised upbringing for all our youngsters merely by stopping a few of the more flagrant assaults on their vulnerable personality. They must also seek to know why those cruelties exist, and having established the reason they must expose it and begin a process of education which will destroy all the illusions and rationalisations surrounding the raising of children.

Adult chauvinism

This will not be easy. Adult dominance is established at the heart of our national life. It has almost exactly the same status as the idea of male supremacy had in the early years of this century, when the suffragettes were fighting for the right to vote, and it is underpinned by a similar rationale. Like the majority of men in those times, who believed without question that being female disqualified you from having an opinion about anything outside the domestic round, adults see no reason to ask themselves whether children need treatment any different from what they receive at present. Like the mass of women before they were given the vote, children have accepted their subordination, and cannot imagine having more rights than they possess at the moment. Consequently, in spite of the anger it often arouses in them they have little choice but to accept, and in the end believe, that the harsh, frequently capricious and even arbitrary control they endure from their parents is right, and no more than they deserve.

Only radical, and therefore uncomfortable, challenges to this state of affairs can hope to succeed. I do not profess to know exactly and in detail how we can go about recasting the image children are forced to bear in our society, but I suspect that at some stage we shall have to do some of the following things:

- Support the EPOCH campaign for corporal punishment of children to be made unlawful.

- Encourage, through social work education, those who stand as advocates for children to use the new principles set out in the Children Act, by virtue of which children are to be consulted, and to have due weight given to their opinions, before any step is taken affecting their lives.

- Challenge more openly all the assumptions which teachers, politicians, social workers and parents use when talking about children, requiring them to justify what they say not by generalisations but by specific, testable evidence.

and, most contentiously,

- Campaign actively for the lowering of the age at which people become able to vote. 16 would be a modest target, followed in due course by 15 and 14.

If this sounds ridiculous, because children are presumed to have no political ideas worth mentioning, we should remember that the same was said about 18 year olds when the voting age was 21. In any case, there is no evidence that the electoral choices made by millions of those who have the vote show any sign of being especially mature. In the early 1980's vast numbers of people in Great Britain voted for the governing party - which was becoming terminally unpopular at the time - simply because its leader had taken the country to war with Argentina. If that had not happened there is every reason to suppose that the voters would have thrown it out at the next election. I suspect that their reasons for voting against it would have included not only dislike of its policies, but also the fact that it was led by a woman, or even that the other side had a more handsome leader, or that they liked red or yellow rather than blue. The point is not that any particular voter thinks on that trivial level, but rather that becoming 18 does not miraculously transform a person from a hopelessly superficial thinker into a serious political philosopher.

In fact, there are many young people who have clear, well thought-out ideas about how the country should be run, ideas formed out of as much good information as any adult possesses. If they had the vote they would be able to exercise it only in favour of one of the three major parties. Since our present system does not allow subtle differences of emphasis in the formulation of policy to express themselves through small parties, elected by proportional representation and able to influence affairs only in alliance with others, the most any large bloc of voters, such as schoolchildren, would be able to achieve with their suffrage would be the implementation of an integral programme selected from a list of three.

The result would be precisely what it is now: the alternation of governments of the left and the right. The only difference would be that those governments would have to listen, as they have never listened before, to the real voice of young people. They would have to recognise that if you treat people high-handedly and force upon them compulsory schooling when they do not want or need it, together with a painful experience of subordination, they are liable to vote against you.

It follows, then, that lowering the voting age will tend to focus the minds of politicians upon issues which they do not have to face at the moment. The knowledge that an M.P.'s political future lies partly in the hands of people whom he has been in the habit of pushing around without consultation cannot fail to impress upon him the need to find out, for the first time, what these people really want, and to start giving it to them.

Strangely enough, I should be surprised if many children of school age, even when endowed with a vote, wanted to abolish schools. The tendency adults have to see children as naturally more interested in triviality and time-wasting than in serious learning, is belied by the almost incredible intellectual feats which all normal children perform before they set foot in a school. They analyse the world around them, and work out that it is divided into discrete entities. They absorb the complex sound-patterns of the language spoken around them, and accurately relate them to those entities.

Soon they are able to use this knowledge to say things, some of which have never been said before. They learn all this accurately and certainly, even if their parents are illiterate, untrained in teaching and innocent of any 'professional' understanding. They need no schooling at this age because their natural zest for living, their uncompromising drive to become more sure of themselves in this amazing world of ours fills them with determination. Even if we did not force them to go to school they would want to learn, and school could become the natural place to do it.

This could only happen if schools were organised in such a way that they did not become centres for the manipulation of unwilling helots. They would have to be made democratic, respectful, tolerant of inexperience, and flexible enough to allow all types of children to become as proficient as they felt able to be. Only in this way could they hope to avoid assailing the children's essential dignity and contributing to the accumulation of pain from which so many evils certainly come.

Inevitably this fundamental alteration of priorities in education will not come about until legislators see it as necessary and valuable. This will not happen until the people affected by it possess the only argument which politicians in a democratic society have to take seriously: the right to decide whether they keep the power they have, or give it up to someone else. Only if children are given that right will they find a way to defend themselves from the thoughtlessness of the adult world.

I once saw children learning through practice to use democracy. It was during a television documentary about Summerhill School. The film crew had been given the run of the school for a whole term, and had been able to film some of the more sensational aspects of its life. Inevitably the film showed a great many events and encounters which would not take place in a State school. Children were seen arguing, shouting, playing loud, energetic games, and taking part in the rough-and-tumble of life in a community in which every individual has a jealously guarded right to say anytime what is on their mind.

To a person used to seeing children sitting in silence while those older than them tell them what to do and what to think, it was an unedifying sight. The newspapers next day were weighed down by reams of righteous indignation from reviewers and readers alike. I looked in vain for signs that anyone had grasped the essential fact about the film, which was that it showed children learning, successfully, to do what most adults in the outside world cannot do: express a point of view, listen to what other people think about it, take part in a democratic response to it, and accept the final decision with a good grace.

I have met Summerhill children, and they have impressed me. They behaved exactly as any ordinary adult person would like to see young people behaving, with dignity and unforced politeness. They had used the school meeting to expose their vehement emotions, and bring them into balance. Outside the school, they were able to restrain themselves and hold their feelings in check. State school pupils seem to do the opposite. They are forced to hold back the natural tide of confused, stormy adolescent self-centredness so that their teachers may feel in command of them. The inescapable consequence - a thoughtful educator would predict it - is that they do all the shouting, arguing and banging the furniture which they need to do, outside the safe confines of the school, often in places and ways which get them into more or less serious trouble.

The price of survival through endurance

All these reflections are my response to Alice Miller's writings. She has pioneered an essential line of development in thinking about the civilised education and socialisation of children. Her books deserve to be read not only because they are liberal and humane, but also because they reveal why, in spite of the technological sophistication we have acquired in Europe, and in spite of our having lived through the most homicidal century there has ever been, we still find a rank growth of unrepentant, motiveless cruelty thrusting itself out from under our feet as we struggle to crush it.

Dr. Miller reveals in all her work the folly of the attitude expressed by a retired psychiatrist (of all people), formerly in charge of a large clinic, who said:

> " 'You needn't get so worked up about child abuse; what you call abuse is something the child can survive without any great difficulty. Children are experts in survival.' In this statement the doctor was doubtless correct, but the tragedy is that he did not know the price of this survival, any more than he knew that he had also paid the price himself and had made others pay. For

> *forty years he had treated female and male patients, prescribed*
> *medication for them, talked encouragingly to them, and never*
> *once grasped that the grave psychotic conditions he was*
> *observing every day were nothing but attempts to describe, in the*
> *language of symptoms, the mistreatments and confusion of their*
> *childhood."*
>
> (*Banished Knowledge - Facing Childhood Injuries* (1990) p.64. Virago)

That 'Language of Symptoms' furnished the vocabulary with which Hitler, Stalin, Ceausescu and many others delivered to mankind their message of savagery. The hidden horror of their mute, helpless suffering became directly manifest in the torment they inflicted without end on whoever cynical convenience placed in their power. The unavoidable choice confronts us: to allow that horror to replicate itself in every generation or to bring it to light and fearlessly destroy it.

We cannot achieve this if we insulate ourselves from the reality which we are trying to reveal to others. Our feelings are part of the persona we offer to our children. Why, then, do we tolerate a culture of child-rearing and education in which emotion is stigmatised and its expression punished? We need urgently to recognise the unreason of allowing most of our children to be brought up by the kind of educator who sees their feelings as either trivial or dangerous, and who really thinks that youngsters learn best how to live with each other by never being allowed to express any emotion which would be out of place at a vicarage garden-party.

I am not optimistic about the possibility of this essential change of outlook coming about, but I am sure that our Society is doomed if it does not. Change will require daring, educators will have to learn that very few of the attitudes they have absorbed and lived by make sense when viewed from outside the structure of contemptuous dogma about children which schools and many parents live by.

For perhaps the first time in human history, adults will have to enter into relationships with children as they really are, and not as those adults believe or want them to be. Alice Miller has shown that the key which unlocks those new relationships is the adults' fearless determination to look into their own childhood and honestly confront what they find there.

Bibliography

Forward S. and Buck C. (1990) *Toxic Parents: Overcoming the legacy of parental abuse*. Bantam Press.

Lifton B.J. (1989) *The King of Children*. Pan Books.

Malkin P. and Stein H. (1990) *Eichmann in my Hands*. Muller.

Miller A. (1986) *Pictures of a Childhood*. Translated by Hildegard and Hunter Hannum. New York: Farrar, Straus and Giroux.

Miller A. (1987) *Prisoners of Childhood*. Translated by Ruth Ward. Reissued in paperback as *The Drama of Being a Child*. Virago.

Miller A. (1987) *For Your Own Good: Hidden cruelty in child-rearing, and the roots of violence*. Translated by Hildegard and Hunter Hannum. Virago.

Miller A. (1987) *Thou Shalt Not Be Aware: Society's betrayal of the child*. Translated by Hildegard and Hunter Hannum. Virago.

Miller A. (1990) *The Untouched Key: Tracing childhood trauma in creativity and destructiveness*. Translated by Hildegard and Hunter Hannum. Virago.

Miller A. (1990) *Banished Knowledge: Facing childhood injuries*. Translated by Leila Vennewitz. Virago.

Miller A. (1991) *Breaking Down the Wall of Silence (To Join the Waiting Child)*. Translated by Simon Worrall. Virago.

Newell P. (1989) *Children Are People Too*. London: Bedford Square Press.

Shute C. (1993) *Compulsory Schooling Disease* Nottingham: Educational Heretics Press

COMPULSORY SCHOOLING DISEASE

After twenty-five years as a modern languages teacher, Chris Shute, in his first book, presents his misgivings about schooling:

"I agreed to write this book because, after twenty-five years of school-teaching I became convinced that I was engaged in a form of microcosmic fascism. I intend to show in this book that schooling is, indeed, an activity which has aspects in common with fascism. That is not to say that teachers mean it to be so, or that they are conscious of the evil in which they are involved. Even fascism in its early phases attracted some reasonable, high-minded people who believed that the world could be changed for the better merely by the use of a little force and rigour in the right place."

"Perhaps their (my fellow teachers) true motivation was summed up for me by a lady colleague of mine some years ago. I had been talking to her about the grey, strained expressions I saw on the faces of my pupils as they went about the school. I suggested that it might be something to do with their feeling that they were not being educated so much as sentenced to hard labour for the crime of being children. She thought for a moment, and said in a grim voice: "I went through it. I see no reason why my child should escape.""

"I cannot bring myself to see education as she (my colleague) saw it, a life-long campaign against spontaneity, liveliness, and the natural energy of youth. Neither can I accept that the anger and frustration I saw in those children, which I now recognise as the same anger that slaves and occupied people feel, serves any good purpose in education."

"Home-based education or home-schooling is not discussed. This is not because I do not take it seriously as a method of educating children. In fact, I believe it is currently the best way to educate most children. But I hope that one day soon it will be possible for children to use schools as they should be used, as places where any person who happens to need help with their studies can go and receive it. Until that time, I must confine myself to commenting on schools as they are now, and challenging us to consider whether their regime contributes to enslaving the minds of children rather than setting them free."

ISBN 0-9518022-1-6   Price £6-00 from: **Educational Heretics Press**
113 Arundel Drive, Bramcote Hills, Nottingham NG9 3FQ

Education Now

EDUCATION NOW thinks that the word *education* has come to be misunderstood. Many people assume that it means 'what teachers do with children in school' and nothing else. **EDUCATION NOW** challenges that view. Its understanding of education is much wider, encompassing the many beneficial experiences which take place outside schools and colleges and which lead to valuable learning. It opposes those elements in the present system which promote uniformity, dependency, and often, a lasting sense of failure.

The vision of **EDUCATION NOW** includes:
- a focus on the uniqueness of individuals, of their learning experiences and of their many and varied learning styles
- support of education in human scale settings including home-based education, small schools, mini-schools, and schools-within-schools, flexischooling and flexi-colleges
- recognition that learners themselves have the ability to make both rational and intuitive choices about their education
- advocacy of co-operative and democratic organisation of places of learning
- belief in the need to share national resources so that everyone has a real choice in education
- acceptance of Einstein's proposal that *imagination is more important than knowledge* in our modern and constantly changing world
- adoption of the Universal Declaration of Human Rights in general and the European Convention for the Protection of Human Rights and Fundamental Freedoms in particular.

EDUCATION NOW maintains that people learn best:
- when they are self-motivated
- when they take responsibility for their own lives and learning
- when they feel comfortable in their surroundings
- when teachers and learners value, trust, respect and listen to each other
- when education is seen as a life-long process

EDUCATION NOW is a forum in which people with differing, diverse and undogmatic views can develop dialogue about alternatives to existing dominant and compulsory forms of education.

Office: 113 Arundel Drive, Bramcote Hills, Nottingham NG9 3FQ

BOOKS BY EDUCATION NOW

Beyond Authoritarian School Management by Lynn Davies £10-00
*...vital reading for anyone keen to move beyond the limitations of
authoritarian school management into more effective forms of practice*

Never Too Late by John Holt £10-00
I applaud this book heartily ... Sir Yehudi Menuhin

Anatomy of Choice in Education Roland Meighan & Philip Toogood £10-00
*...precisely what is needed to clear up present confusion and set coherent,
purposeful, productive patterns for the future...* Dr. James Hemming

Democratic Learning and Learning Democracy by Clive Harber £5-00
Democracy is the worst system of organisation - except for all the others!
Winston Churchill

Learning From Home-based Education edited by Roland Meighan £5-00
...the rich diversity of the home-based phenomenon is demonstrated.

Issues in Green Education by Damian Randle £5-00
... it certainly succeeds in provoking thought ... Chris Hartnett

Sharing Power in Schools: Raising Standards by Bernard Trafford £5-00
*... our students are becoming more effective, self-confident and imaginative
learners and workers. Examination results are improving ...*

Early Childhood Education: Taking Stock
edited by Philip Gammage and Janet Meighan £5-00
This is essential reading for all involved in the education of young children.

Community Need and Further Education edited by Frank Reeves £10-00
The application of the principles of community education in a college of F.E.

Skills for Self-managed learning by Mike Roberts £5-00
This book reports on a ten year research study into this topic

Education Now, 113 Arundel Drive, Bramcote Hills, Nottingham NG9 3FQ